VIKINGS 50

All-Time Greatest Players in Franchise History

Jim Bruton

TRIUMPH
BOOKS

Library of Congress Cataloging-in-Publication Data

Bruton, James H., 1945–
Vikings 50 : all-time greatest players in franchise history / Jim Bruton.
p. cm.
ISBN 978-1-60078-691-4 (hardback)
1. Minnesota Vikings (Football team)—History. 2. Football players—United States—Biography. I. Title. II. Title: Vikings fifty.
GV956.M5.B88 2012
796.332'6409776579—dc23
2012014027

This book is available in quantity at special discounts for your group or organization. For further information, contact:

Triumph Books LLC
814 North Franklin Street
Chicago, Illinois 60610
(312) 337-0747
www.triumphbooks.com

Printed in China
ISBN: 978-1-60078-691-4

Design by Patricia Frey
All photos courtesy of the Minnesota Vikings unless otherwise noted

To my wonderful wife of 42 years, Mary; my beloved children—Jim, Dan, and Molly; my amazing daughters-in-law Sandra and Janelle and my incredible son-in-law Patrick; my very special grandchildren—Michael, Alexandra, Nicholas, Ellysa, and Annalise; and to Abbi (my golden retriever).

I love you all more than you will ever know.

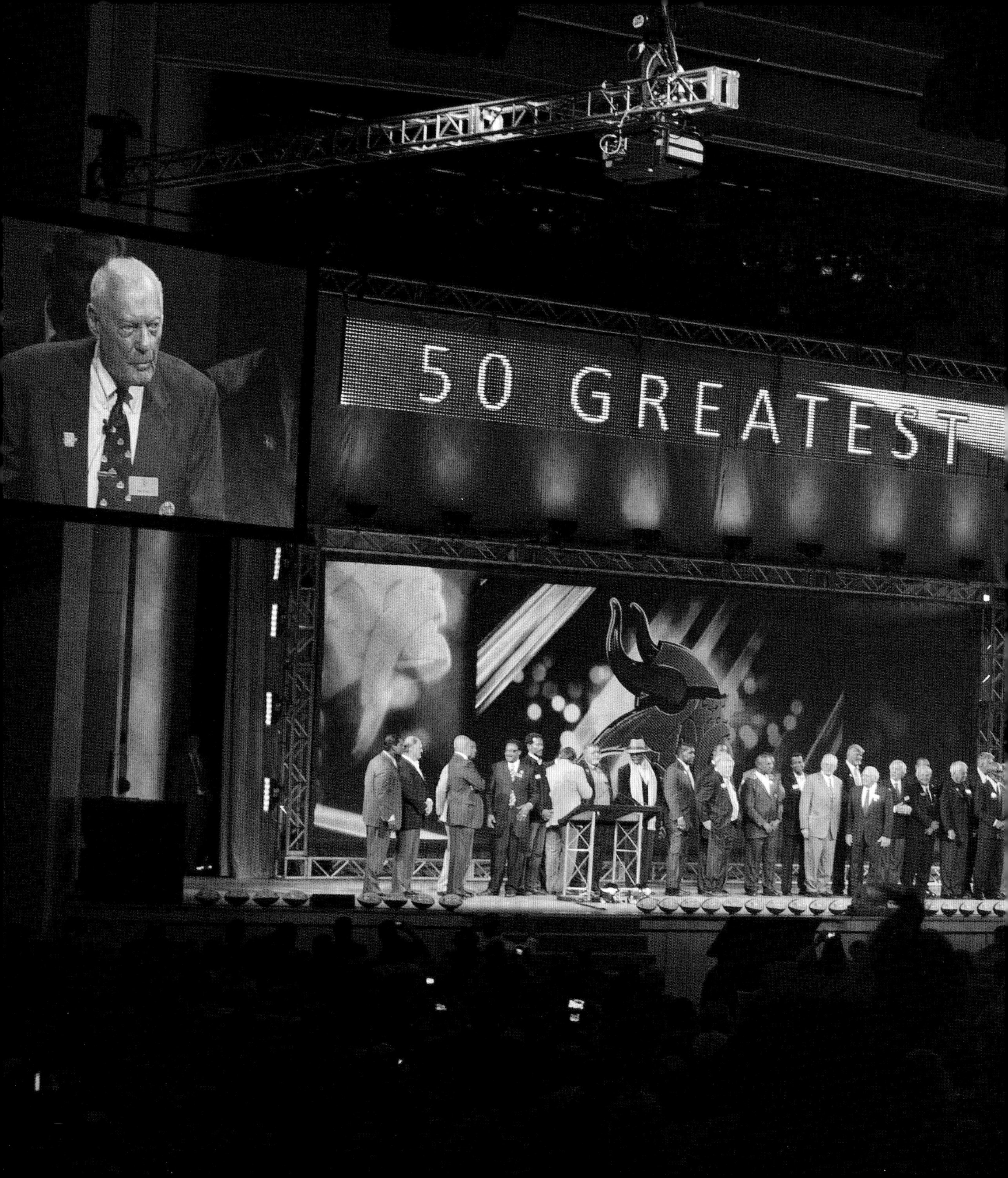
50 GREATEST

Contents

Tarkenton eyes one of his favorite targets, Chuck Foreman, during game action.

Foreword

I feel so fortunate to have put on the Vikings jersey at the team's very first practice, which was held in Bemidji, Minnesota, in the summer of 1961. To be present at the beginning of the franchise's existence was one of the great thrills of my life, and I'm so proud that I am part of the team's history. Looking back and remembering the team's amazing growth, greatest triumphs, and all of the great players reminds me of what a blessing it is to be a Viking.

From its humble origins as an expansion team in 1961, the Vikings have gone on to become one of the great franchises in all of professional sports. I will always be able to look back and say that I was there from day one. I know how hard the players and coaches worked to get from an expansion franchise to 18 division championships and four Super Bowl appearances.

Perhaps above all, I am grateful to have played for such great coaches as Bud Grant and Jerry Burns. These men shaped my life and helped me become the man I am today. I learned so much from them—and some of it was even about football! I learned what it meant and what it takes to be a leader. I learned how to pay attention and look for the signs that others overlook, the little things that are actually big. I'm forever grateful for the impact they had on me and my career, and I know my former teammates would say the same.

Of course, being part of a team doesn't end with the men on the sideline. It's also a lifelong relationship with fans and supporters, people who come out to watch and cheer on the team every week. I've been around professional football for 50 years, and I have never found a fan base more passionate and loyal than the fans of the Minnesota Vikings. We could always count on them—no matter how bitter-cold it was! The fans were always a great inspiration to me and my teammates, and I never cease to be amazed at how many Vikings fans I run into, no matter where I am in the country.

To be selected as one of the 50 greatest Vikings is one of the biggest honors of my life. Since that first day, I have either played with or watched every player who has worn the Vikings jersey—and there have been plenty of extraordinary ones to see! We had so many off-the-charts, incredible players on the Vikings teams on which I played—great players and great people who have become lifelong friends. And the list of noteworthy Vikings has only grown longer in the years since my retirement in 1978.

The stories of the 50 exceptional, legendary players in this book will stir your soul. Enjoy!

—Fran Tarkenton

50 Years of the MINNESOTA VIKINGS

1961

Norm Van Brocklin became the Minnesota Vikings' first head coach in franchise history, beginning the 1961 season. Van Brocklin—who the previous year had led the Philadelphia Eagles *on the field*, as quarterback—had never coached before. He was given the Herculean task of forming a new team and making them competitive in the National Football League.

It didn't take long, as the upstart Vikings managed a colossal upset in the first game of the 1961 season, defeating the "Mighty Monsters of the Midway," the Chicago Bears, by a score of 37–13. It remains one of the greatest upsets in the history of the National Football League, and the victory established the notoriety of a football team clad in purple, with horns on the sides of their helmets.

That game was more than just a victory. It was the beginning of an 18-year Hall of Fame career for one of the greatest quarterbacks in the history of the game: Francis Asbury Tarkenton.

1964

The Van Brocklin era had its stormy times, and some great wins along the way. It also featured some legendary players in its early years, such as the great Hugh McElhenny, who finished his brilliant career in Minnesota. McElhenny later was inducted into the Pro Football Hall of Fame.

1967

By the time the decade came to a close, Van Brocklin was gone and Bud Grant—former star player at the University of Minnesota and head coach of the often-champion Winnipeg Blue Bombers of the Canadian Football League—was hired to lead the franchise.

With some outstanding players in place, like center Mick Tingelhoff, running backs Bill "Boom Boom" Brown and Dave Osborn, and others, including Jim Marshall, Grady Alderman, Carl Eller, Fred Cox, and so many more, Grant was able to use his sound coaching expertise and skilled management of players to build the foundation for a championship team.

A Timeline

1969

Grant had put together a championship-caliber club and took his team all the way to the Super Bowl in 1969. The Vikings fell 23–7 to the Kansas City Chiefs, but it began the run of divisional championships and Super Bowls in the 1970s.

1972

The Vikings had traded Fran Tarkenton to the New York Giants before the 1967 season, but the quarterback's return for the 1972 campaign was the final piece of the puzzle for the team that had built its foundation piece by piece over the last decade.

1973

The Vikings of the 1970s will long be remembered for their defenses, led by the famed "Purple People Eaters" front four—Jim Marshall, Alan Page, Carl Eller, and Gary Larsen, and later, Doug Sutherlund.

The Vikings dominated the National Football League in the 1970s with Super Bowl appearances in 1973, 1974, and 1976. It could have been four consecutive years, but the team was halted in the 1975 NFC divisional playoff game by a non-call—a flagrant "push-off" that was clearly pass interference—in a loss to the Dallas Cowboys. It was one of the most devastating losses in franchise history, and it derailed one of the best Vikings teams ever put together.

1979

By the end of the decade, Fran Tarkenton had retired, and the Vikings were led into the 1980s by a budding young signal caller from Texas named Tommy Kramer. Some of the other veteran players were also retiring, and the Vikings were beginning their first major facelift in many seasons. It had been a monumental decade of Vikings football.

1982

Perhaps the biggest change for the Vikings, beyond the retirement of head coach Bud Grant, was the surroundings, as the team moved from its cold and frigid home at Metropolitan Stadium in Bloomington to the consistent temperature and hooded roof of the Metrodome in downtown Minneapolis.

During these years, the team saw the emergence of some great players in linebacker Scott Studwell, Kramer, running back Ted Brown, and their two outstanding receivers from the past decade, Ahmad Rashad and Sammy White.

1984

The Vikings suffered along with the retirement of Grant. The one-season run of former assistant Les Steckel was disastrous, and calls for the return of Grant in an effort to stabilize the franchise after a disappointing 3–13 season under Steckel were rampant. Order was returned to the organization in 1985 with the single-season return of Grant, and the team was primed for the emergence of new head coach and longtime Vikings offensive coordinator Jerry Burns, who took over for the 1986 season.

1986

The mid-1980s and beyond were highlighted by some great moments in team history from such outstanding players as wide receiver Anthony Carter and quarterback Tommy Kramer. Defensive end and future Hall of Famer Chris Doleman, defensive back Joey Browner, and defensive tackle Keith Millard were outstanding players on the other side of the ball. Running back Darrin Nelson and future Hall of Fame offensive tackle Gary Zimmerman led the team to some great season finishes.

1989

The decade also marked the infamous trade of running back Herschel Walker from the Dallas Cowboys to Minnesota—in exchange for multiple high draft picks and several players. Walker had been a superior running back in college and in professional football, but for whatever reason, he was unable to capture his prominence in purple and gold. General manager Mike Lynn had felt the Vikings only needed to fill one position—running back—to bring back its championship prominence. He felt Walker was that back. And although Herschel was a tremendous person and teammate, he was never able to deliver the vision.

1992

Dennis Green was hired as the head coach for the 1992 season and provided the Vikings with leadership on the field while delivering a lot of wins along the way. The Vikings saw a number of prominent starters from other teams make their way to Minnesota. Players like Jim McMahon, formerly of the Chicago Bears, and Warren Moon of the Houston Oilers left their mark on some good seasons wearing the Purple. Fans also were in awe of the greatness of running back Robert Smith and the emergence of future Hall of Famers, lineman John Randle and guard Randall McDaniel, two of the best to ever play the game during the decade.

1998

In 1998, Randy Moss arrived. Randall Cunningham, former Philadelphia Eagles quarterback, led the Vikings that memorable season. He took over for the injured Brad Johnson, and with Moss and Cris Carter at the receiving end of most passes, the team seemed untouchable. It became one of the franchise's greatest seasons ever; the team posted some of the highest offensive numbers in NFL history. Unfortunately, the fabulous run was spoiled by a devastating playoff loss to the Atlanta Falcons.

2001

Dennis Green was gone as head coach after the 2001 season, and former player and assistant coach Mike Tice took the reins. Fans were delighted by the continuing play of Randy Moss and the skills of quarterback Daunte Culpepper, who put together some phenomenal seasons.

The team also suffered through some tough times both on and off the field—the worst being the death of offensive lineman Korey Stringer during training camp in 2001. It was as difficult a time as anything the franchise had ever faced.

The Vikings were also shaken by the sudden retirement of running back Robert Smith and the loss via free agency of offensive cornerstone tackle Todd Steussie. Cris Carter, one of the best receivers in franchise history, soon retired. Randy Moss was traded, returned, and was unceremoniously traded again, as the decade moved toward its conclusion.

2006

New ownership took over the Vikings, ultimately leading to the dismissal of Mike Tice and the arrival of new head coach Brad Childress. During his four-plus years at the helm, Childress improved upon the team's record, culminating in a valiant run at the Super Bowl with former Green Bay Packer Brett Favre at quarterback in 2009.

2010

Favre's second season in Purple, fraught with injury and turbulence, ended the reign of Childress in midseason. And to top off the season of despair, the Metrodome roof collapsed under the weight of a massive snowstorm, requiring the Vikings and their new coach Leslie Frasier to play two of their home games at the Minnesota Gophers' TCF Bank Stadium and in Michigan at the Detroit Lions' home field.

Despite a record-tying worst season of only three wins in 2011, things are looking up for the Vikings. With the likes of Jared Allen rushing the passer in record numbers and (hopefully) Adrian Peterson returning to form after suffering a season-ending knee injury in 2011, there is a lot to look forward to. Linebacker Chad Greenway, tight end Kyle Rudolph, center John Sullivan, and solid defensive tackle Kevin Williams are just a few players whose futures look bright. And with Christian Ponder and Joe Webb vying for the quarterback position, the future *is* bright.

Where it all happens.

Coach Norm Van Brocklin poses with some of the Vikings' early recruits, including soon-to-be-superstar Fran Tarkenton (10).

Introduction

My connection to the Minnesota Vikings goes back almost 50 years. In the fall of 1963, I was just 18 years old when I approached Norm Van Brocklin as he walked off the practice field at the old and long-since-gone Midway Stadium in St. Paul. "I can kick a football farther than anyone you have," I brazenly told "the Dutchman."

From there, after an unofficial tryout with the Purple the following spring, I got a favorable recommendation to the University of Minnesota—where I played sparingly, to say the least. A few games, a couple of tackles, and some points in the annual spring game were my collegiate claim to fame.

Later, after some free-agent tryout camps, I landed with the Vikings and signed contracts for the 1967 and 1971 seasons; I also signed with the Dallas Cowboys in 1968. I was among early training-camp cuts each year, but I will never forget that big-league atmosphere.

One of my fondest memories was receiving a photo from Bud Grant, which he sent to me many years later. The image is instantly recognizable—you know, the one with Bud on the sideline, headset in place, standing erect. But it's not the photo that I am so enamored with, it's the notation he wrote on it: "To Jim, I always wished you would have tried out again, so I could have cut you three times."

It didn't matter that I was cut in training camp. What mattered was that Bud took the time to send it to me. He means so much to me even today. Just to be in camp and to be cut by Bud, not once but twice, was pretty special.

Forty-six years' worth of season tickets might also be an indication of how I feel about the team. I was there the very first game in franchise history—and saw rookie quarterback Fran Tarkenton come off the bench and throw four touchdown passes and run for another, to beat the Chicago Bears.

There have been a lot of games since—regular-season matchups, playoffs, and four Super Bowls. It has been a wonderful ride. To write *Vikings 50: All-Time Greatest Players in Franchise History* has been a tremendous honor. I sincerely hope it is as enjoyable to read as it has been for me to write.

Author's Note

In 2010, the Minnesota Vikings celebrated their 50th anniversary as a franchise in the National Football League. To mark the occasion, they asked fans to vote for the team's 50 greatest all-time players. In a ceremony held at the Minneapolis Convention Center in December, the Vikings' 50 greatest were announced and the players were introduced. At the final home game of the season, the honored Vikings again appeared before their fans to receive the distinction.

What follows is an accounting of the Vikings' chosen 50, the greatest players ever to wear the Purple. Many of them were generous in providing me with their personal recollections on playing for the franchise, as well as offering personal photographs for this book.

Their feats on the field are well known to every dyed-in-the-wool Minnesota fan. What you will find in this book are the men who transcend the gridiron.

Jubilant players hoist coach and fellow honoree Bud Grant at the 50 greatest Vikings halftime ceremony.

In 2010, the Minnesota Vikings celebrated their 50th anniversary as a franchise in the National Football League.

The 50 Vikings honorees gather at TCF Bank Stadium on the University of Minnesota campus, where the Vikings played their second regular-season matchup against the Chicago Bears.

Posing for a portrait photo during training camp.

"Grady was an extremely smart football player. He had superior technique."

—JERRY BURNS

Grady ALDERMAN

#67 | Offensive Tackle, 1961–74

Grady Alderman was a dominant force on the offensive line for the Minnesota Vikings from the inception of the franchise. His 16 years in the NFL were highlighted by magnificent line play, as he was selected to play in five Pro Bowls. Alderman came to the Vikings as one of the expansion-draft players for the team's opening season in 1961. Classified as one of head coach Norm Van Brocklin's "stiffs" (players sent to him who teams didn't want), Alderman proved everyone wrong. He became a fixture on the offensive line.

Alderman grew up in the housing projects of Detroit. He didn't have the opportunity to play organized sports until he was in the 10th grade, when his family moved out of the projects to Madison Heights, a suburb of Detroit. His father worked in the automobile industry in Detroit as an inspector. "All we did was play sports in the housing projects," remembers Alderman. "We would have two to three players on a side and go at it. By suppertime, we usually had enough for full teams." It was the lure of sports that captured Alderman. And by the time he got into the organized-sports arena, he excelled at his major interest.

Grady played football for three years in high school and also thrived as a basketball player. While in high school, he became friends with Jim Meyers, who became known in the world of professional wrestling as George "the Animal" Steele. The two have continued the friendship through the decades. Alderman was an outstanding offensive and defensive lineman, earning offers at Hillsdale College (Michigan) and Michigan State University, but he chose to stay close to home and attended the University of Detroit, now Detroit Mercy.

While attending college he received a degree in accounting. Although he had his sights set on playing professionally, he knew that even if he was good enough to make a team, it wouldn't be forever, and he needed a foundation for a career after the game ended.

His prowess as an offensive lineman at Detroit Mercy got him enough recognition from the professional football ranks that he was selected as the 111th pick in the 1960 NFL Draft, going to the Detroit Lions in the 10th round. He made the Lions roster in 1960 before being selected in the following year's expansion draft by the Minnesota Vikings. He was one of eight players who the Lions exposed for the draft and one of three ultimately selected by the Vikings.

At first, Grady was disappointed to leave Detroit, but he soon decided it would be for the best; he was excited to be a part of a brand-new football franchise. His optimism quickly faded.

4

In 1963, Alderman recovered four fumbles during the season, a team high and fourth among all NFL players that year.

"The first year with Minnesota and Coach Van Brocklin was awful," recalls Alderman. "The second year, well, I guess we just didn't know any better. They ran so many players through camp that first year, it was hard to know who was coming and who was going. I think there must have been 75 to 100 players in camp. As for me, I wasn't smart enough at the time to know if I was doing well or if I was on the way out.

"I remember Jim Marshall came to us from Cleveland. He had been ill and was down to about 212 pounds. Jim eventually got well and became a great player for the Vikings for two decades."

"Grady was as sound a football player as was ever made, a terrific offensive lineman and as steady as a rock."

—FRAN TARKENTON

Alderman survived the early years and became a fixture on teams that boasted some of the greatest Vikings players of all time. Legendary names like Fran Tarkenton, Mick Tingelhoff, Bill Brown, Dave Osborn, Ron Yary, the Purple People Eaters, and others defined the franchise's glorified history.

There were only a few promising years in the Van Brocklin era, but all that would change when Bud Grant became the head coach in 1967. *Everything* changed with the arrival of Grant. It didn't take him long to mold his team and solid contributors like Grady Alderman into championship players.

Alderman served as team captain for the Vikings for eight seasons and was a leader on and off the field. He was a master at preparation, studying each opponent and utilizing his game smarts and overall quickness.

Alderman's final year with the Vikings was in 1974. A shift in the roster size doomed his chance to continue with the Vikings, but he sought a final year in the NFL with the Chicago Bears and his former Vikings general manager

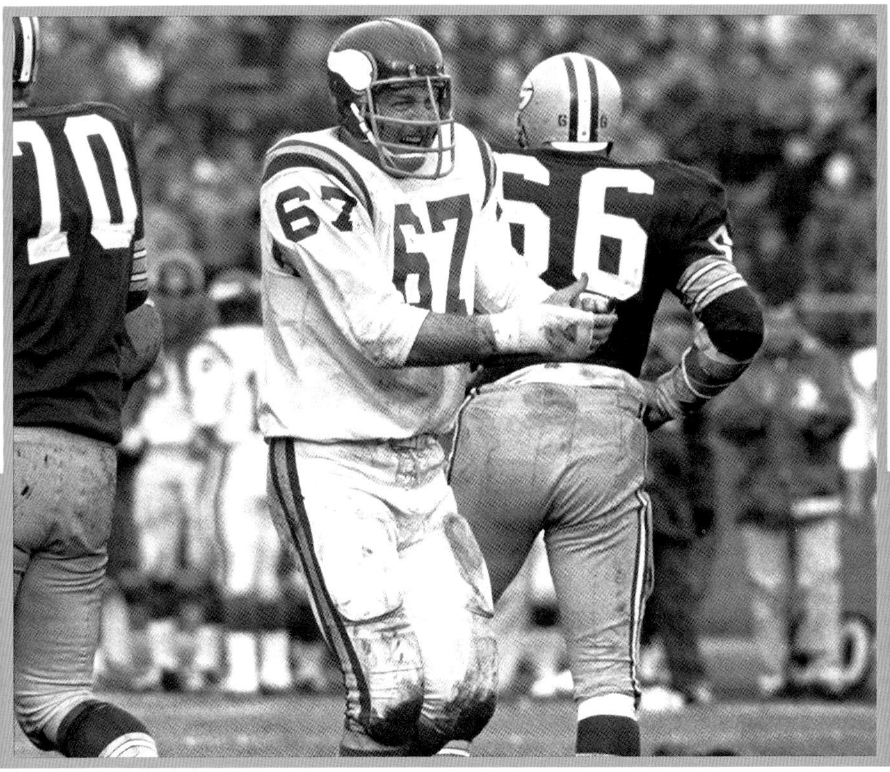

Alderman celebrates during play against the Green Bay Packers.

Jim Finks. After becoming a casualty in the Bears' final cut, the decision to retire became easy for the wily veteran.

In 1960, when the Detroit Lions didn't put stock in his abilities as a player and put him on the expansion block, they were dead wrong. For 14 seasons, Alderman was the anchor on the Minnesota Vikings offensive line, earning him a place in 2010 among the 50 greatest Vikings. "It meant a lot to me to be selected," he says. "The best way to say it is, it makes me very proud of my years with the Vikings."

After his football career came to an end, Grady went into broadcasting and was the color commentator for Minnesota Vikings football for four seasons on WCCO radio. "Fran Tarkenton got me into the broadcasting business," he recalls. "We became very good friends, and Fran called the station manager at WCCO radio and put in a good word for me. I was on the radio doing Vikings games for four seasons and worked alongside Joel McConnel and Ray Scott, both outstanding radio men."

After the announcing job, Alderman went to work in the Vikings front office with team general manager Mike Lynn. "I had a background in accounting, so I was helpful to Mike in this area and was very much involved in the construction at the Metrodome and the construction of the team's Winter Park complex."

He left the Twin Cities in 1981 to become the general manager of the Denver Broncos. "It was my old friend Fran Tarkenton helping me out with this job also," says Alderman. "He was always there for me and still is today. We have retained a wonderful friendship through the years."

Alderman spent only one season with the Broncos in the general manager role. It was the end of Alderman's career in football but the beginning of a new life in one of the most beautiful parts of the United States, Evergreen, Colorado, where he makes his home.

The NFL is plenty different than it was in Alderman's day. The players are bigger, faster, stronger, and make a lot more money these days. Alderman played at 6'2" and 245 pounds, the size of some running backs nowadays. He made $60,000 at the top of his career and a paltry $8,000 during his first professional contract. But Grady Alderman is a proud and thankful man and a wonderful representative of the Minnesota Vikings.

The Alderman family.
Photo courtesy of Grady Alderman

Jared ALLEN

#69 | Defensive End, 2008–Present

Before Jared Allen is done playing professional football, he may become the most prolific pass-rushing defensive end in the history of the game. He has the physical gifts and perfect personality for the position: speed, power, and an internal motor that never stops running. During the 2011 season, Allen set the Vikings' all-time sack record and was just one shy of the NFL record.

"I quit all [other] sports when I was just a kid, about eight years old," says Allen. "I seriously wanted to concentrate on football. My father had a professional tryout with the Minnesota Vikings, and my brother played, so I knew it was what I wanted to do."

Allen was born in Dallas, Texas, and was raised in the northern part of California, where his father was a rancher. He went to Los Gatos High School for one year and then transferred to Live Oak High School in Morgan Hill, California. While at Live Oak, Allen was named First-Team All-League and Defensive Player of the Year. He also made the First-Team All–Central Coast Section selection.

Jared played college football at Idaho State, where he was in the starting lineup for 33 of 41 games during his collegiate career. He made the All-Conference Team for the Big Sky Conference three times and finished his outstanding college career with 250 tackles, 38.5 sacks, three touchdowns, and three interceptions. As a senior at Idaho State he won the Buck Buchanan Award, given to the most outstanding defensive player in the NCAA Division IAA.

Allen was selected in the fourth round of the 2004 NFL Draft by the Kansas City Chiefs, where he played for four seasons before being traded to the Minnesota Vikings. His superlatives in the past decade are indisputable.

Off the field of play, Allen is equally thrill-seeking; he has done such extraordinary things as hunting wild boar, running with the bulls, and skydiving.

"I've been to Egypt and seen the Great Pyramids, traveled to many places in Europe, and hunted just about everything there is to hunt," says Allen, who gets excited talking about his unusual lifestyle. And of course, on Sundays in the fall, he hunts NFL quarterbacks.

"I know where my gifts athletically came from, and I need to take advantage of every opportunity that I have in life," Allen says. "Take football, for instance. I didn't come into the National Football League to be a backup. My goal is to work hard every day and every game so as to not let the team down. I play eternally for Christ. He gave me these abilities, and I cannot let him down either.

"I have studied the game and others who have succeeded. When I was in Kansas City I used to spend a lot

Allen's intensity makes him a truly fearsome opponent.

"He may be the best pass rusher of all time."

—LESLIE FRAZIER

of time watching Tony Gonzalez work to be a better player every day. Tony is one of the best tight ends to ever play the game, and his work ethic is incredible. I played with him for four years and became soundly convinced that great athletes are not successful by accident. It comes from hard work and preparation," says Allen.

"I had a lot of heroes growing up," says Allen, "and they were all hard workers. I used to watch Jack Youngblood, Roger Craig, Tom Rathman…they were all hard workers. I realized that there are a lot of ways to measure the ability of athletes, but the one thing you cannot measure is their hearts.

"I was very impressed by Herm Edwards, my coach at Kansas City, who always said he would rather have a team made up of good men than great athletes," remarks Allen. "Character is important!"

With his football career in full bloom and an active off-the-field lifestyle, he is even more engaged and passionate when talking about his commitment to his charity work. Allen has been a longtime supporter of veterans and started the Jared Allen Homes for Wounded Warriors charity in 2010. It is a nonprofit organization with a mission "to provide financial assistance and support to our injured United States military veterans by building handicapped-accessible homes to suit their individual needs—one wounded warrior at a time," he says.

The Homes for Wounded Warriors initiative was created by Allen after he returned home from a USO tour of military bases in the Middle East. Allen says that he made a commitment to say thank you to all those who had given of themselves to protect our freedom, and he found a way to do this with the start of his organization. His goal is to make a positive, life-changing experience for those who are the most in need and to make their lives easier.

The core concept of the charity is Allen's belief that when a person comes home he needs to feel safe and comfortable: "a place to be yourself," he says. A great example of Allen's efforts can be found in the case of veteran Josh Bullis. A triple amputee, Bullis lost both legs and an arm while serving in Afghanistan in August 2010. Through Homes for Wounded Warriors, Bullis has gained back some of his independence. He was the recipient in his newly purchased home of a wheelchair-accessible shower, wider doorways, lowered countertops, and ramps throughout the home. He is learning to walk again with the help of new prosthetic legs. Bullis has also spent some time with the Vikings as a special guest, sat in on team meetings, and met several of Allen's teammates.

To fund the charity, Allen created a golf outing called Night Ops Charity Golf Outing. Allen was determined to make the event different from other tournaments. And he sure did! For instance, Marines stationed on each hole scream at golfers during their backswings, making shots a little more difficult. And on top of all this, if players happen to hit a bad shot, they are penalized with a round of push-ups. Allen also set up a Slip 'N Slide on one of the holes for anyone who doesn't hit

Allen clowns around with a member of the U.S. armed forces during a USO visit.

Allen pressures former teammate and Seattle quarterback Tarvaris Jackson during a preseason matchup.

the green in regulation. To top it all off, the event begins in the late afternoon, so the back nine is played in the dark. Only an event hosted by Jared Allen could have all these special sidelights.

Allen is a man of astounding character and the highest of beliefs. He has developed a sound philosophy that he tries to live to the fullest every day of his life. "I want to be a God-fearing man, faithful to my wife and family. I have trust in the Lord while living life to the fullest every single day. I will always have full love for my family while taking advantage of every opportunity in life, never thinking that I have finally arrived. I want to never stop developing as a person and hope to apply all of my life's experiences to become a better man. I want to be remembered as someone more than a football player," says Allen.

11

Talk about fearsome. Allen holds the NFL record for consecutive games with a sack, with 11.

Matt Birk anchors the line against the Arizona Cardinals.

Matt BIRK

#75/#78 | Center, 1998–2004, 2006–08

You almost can't make up a story like this. "I'm just Matt Birk, the chubby freckle-faced kid," he says. "Sometimes I can't believe what has happened to me with my career. I truly feel what a privilege it is for me to drive to work every day and play professional football."

Matt Birk attended Cretin High School in St. Paul and was an outstanding student in addition to being an exceptional athlete. He starred in football, basketball, and track and won All-State honors in football and basketball. Academically, he did well enough to earn entrance to Harvard.

Recalling his childhood, he says, "I played all the time, and I told my parents early on that I wanted to be a professional basketball player and play in the NBA. I never gave a thought to professional football [as a kid], let alone playing for our hometown team, the Minnesota Vikings."

Even though Birk was at the center of neighborhood activities throughout most of his young life, his parents also kept him focused on education. He was recruited by some of the Ivy League schools and the service academies, ultimately settling on Harvard to further his athletic and academic goals. While pursuing a degree in economics, professional football was not even on his radar screen until his senior year.

It was a professional scout from the Blesto Scouting Service who told Birk that he had a chance to be drafted by a National Football League team. Birk was selected in the sixth round of the 1998 NFL Draft by the Minnesota Vikings.

"After my senior season at Harvard, I thought I might have a chance to play professionally," says Birk. "Mike Tice, who was the offensive line coach of the Vikings back then, told me he thought I would probably get drafted, but I never gave a thought that I might be picked by Minnesota. It was only a dream. And then it came true." As a Minnesota native, Birk had grown up following the team.

After the NFL Draft, Birk made the team and began gaining the confidence of head coach Dennis Green and Tice. "I knew I didn't need to play right away, and I was determined to learn the game from my coaches. Mike Tice had confidence in me, always gave it to me straight-up, and after two seasons as a backup player, I became Mike Tice's guy. They moved me to the center position, and I have remained there for the past 12 years, the last three with the Baltimore Ravens," says Birk.

In 2000 he took over the starting center role and played every game for the next four seasons. Sidelined by injuries in 2004 and 2005, he returned in 2006 to his familiar center spot and earned another Pro Bowl selection, tying former great Vikings center Mick Tingelhoff for the most Pro Bowl appearances by a Vikings center. Overall, he was selected to play in the Pro Bowl six times and was on the All-Pro Team twice. Quite a feat for someone who had never played center until the pros.

Birk would likely say that his football accolades pale in comparison to his selection as the winner of the Ed Block Courage Award. The award—named in memory of Ed Block, a humanitarian and former trainer of the Baltimore Colts—is given annually to selected players in the NFL who are voted by their teammates as role models of "inspiration, sportsmanship, and courage." The annual selection process is made by the Ed Block Courage Award Foundation, which promotes the prevention of child abuse by raising awareness of the problem and the assisting agencies that provide care and treatment for abused children. His diligence and commitment to community service also won him six consecutive Man of the Year Awards from the Vikings.

The Birk family.
Photo courtesy of Matt Birk

6
In 2007, Birk tied Mick Tingelhoff for the most Pro Bowl appearances by a Vikings center, with six.

Birk has taken a leadership role in the community through his HIKE Foundation (Hope, Inspiration, Knowledge, Education). HIKE was established by the Vikings All-Pro center, in his words, "to provide at-risk children with the educational opportunities needed to excel in the classroom and in life. The foundation impacts the lives of at-risk children by providing interactive programs and resources needed to guide a child through the key educational transitions between elementary, middle, high school, and college." In 2011, Birk received the coveted Walter Payton Man of the Year Award.

Birk is determined to make a difference in the lives of young people. Once, while still with the Vikings, Birk explained the significance of the end zone to a group of young people who had gathered on the practice field at Winter Park, the team complex and home of the Vikings. In addition to pointing out the stripes and distance between the front and back lines, Birk remarked to the group, "As big as it is, you would think we would get in there more often!"

> **"Matt is a lunch-pail-type guy with a tremendous work ethic. If you are playing opposite Matt, you better be ready on every snap of the ball, or he will beat you. He never takes a play off and always has the desire and motivation to outplay his opponents. He is a fantastic leader and sets a great example for young players."**
>
> —LESLIE FRAZIER

His anecdote illustrated to the children the importance of hard work to reaching goals, even those that seem difficult to achieve.

In addition to his strong leadership in the community, Birk has been devoted to keeping his body in shape, no doubt a factor in his long tenure in the NFL. "I have always worked my tail off," says Matt, "in order to stay in shape mentally and physically. I have always thought of my role as a professional football player as not just a job but a lifestyle. I really believe I have lasted 14 years in the NFL because of the way I have taken care of myself with regular training and plenty of rest."

When Birk left the Vikings, it was a shock to the fans and his teammates. Although he has enjoyed his years with the Baltimore Ravens, the Twin Cities is his home and where he will reside in the future. Leaving Minnesota "was the hardest thing I have ever done," he says. "But looking back on the decision, I'm glad we did it, and it was truly a wonderful experience for me and my family. Going to Baltimore revitalized me and my career, and it has been a good thing, but I will be back home again someday."

Of his inclusion among the 50 greatest Minnesota Vikings, he says, " I remember as a youngster hurrying home from church on Sunday for the Vikings game. So to be named one of the 50 greatest, it is an honor that almost doesn't seem right to me. It is just too unbelievable to fathom. With all the great players selected, I'm not sure I am deserving," he says humbly. He is deserving, indeed.

Birk readies for the snap during game action with the Vikings.

Matt BLAIR

#59 | Linebacker, 1974–85

Here comes the snap from center...the ball is down...the kick is up...AND IT'S BLOCKED! BLOCKED BY MATT BLAIR AND THE VIKINGS!

It's a phrase that must have been repeated countless times into the microphones from broadcast play-by-play commentators doing Minnesota Vikings football games on radio and television. Matt Blair blocking kicks wasn't just an occasional fluke; he made a career out of it.

Growing up with a father in the military, Matt traveled the world. Though Hawaii is his official birthplace, his roots were never really established at a single location. As a young athlete, it made it difficult for him to establish a foothold in any sport.

"We didn't have a lot of money when I was growing up," remembers Matt. "I knew if I wanted to attend college, I was going to have to get a scholarship. I was never able to settle into any type of organized sports because we [moved] so often. It seemed like we would always arrive at a new place just as school was starting each year. I played some Pop Warner football, but it was really when I was a junior in high school that I was in competition on a regular basis," says Matt.

Despite difficulties, he was a three-sport athlete, playing basketball, baseball, and participating in track, in which he made the All-City Team. Later, he went on to excel at Northeastern Oklahoma, where he earned a partial scholarship. "I really worked to get that partial scholarship," he continues. "I trained hard and had to compete with 176 others for three scholarships. One of the things we had to do was run a mile—and I did it in five minutes and five seconds, which really impressed the coaches.

"In the end, I received only a partial scholarship. I went out for the basketball team also, and by my second year I had a tremendous growth spurt. I grew two and a half inches and put on more than 40 pounds. I was now at six feet, five inches tall, and I weighed 240 pounds. I was able to really excel and contribute and [then went] to college at Iowa State," says Matt.

In his very first season at Iowa State after transferring from junior college in Oklahoma, Blair was named Defensive Player of the Game in the 1971 Sun Bowl. He also excelled in basketball at the junior-college level.

At one point, Blair was projected to be the first linebacker selected in the 1973 NFL Draft. A knee injury that had sidelined Blair allowed him another season at Iowa

Matt Blair goes for the sack against Lions quarterback Gary Danielson.

State, but it also kept him from becoming a higher draft pick the following year.

In the 1974 NFL Draft, Blair was taken as the 51st pick overall by the Minnesota Vikings. He remained with the team as an outstanding player for 12 seasons. He was selected to play in six consecutive Pro Bowls and also played for the Vikings in two Super Bowls.

During his years with Minnesota, he was known not only as an outstanding defensive player but was also recognized throughout the league as one of the best players in the NFL at blocking punts, field goals, and extra-point kicks. In Super Bowl IX against the Pittsburgh Steelers, Blair blocked a punt that was recovered for a Minnesota Vikings touchdown.

"I believe it was my basketball abilities, the ability to really leap into the air, that helped me so much in being able to block kicks," says Blair. "I loved the challenge."

In addition to his tremendous kick-blocking specialty, he has the distinction of being the only Vikings starter who played on every one of the special teams. He was an outstanding linebacker who excelled at making big plays in big games.

After football, Blair pursued his true passion in photography; he specializes in nature and wildlife. "I have loved doing this kind of work," he says. "It started when I was in my rookie year with the Vikings and we would travel a lot, eight times a season to different cities. So I started taking pictures. I have taught myself the art and strive to take great photos.

"My work really caught on when I met John Chilcott at the Union Gospel Mission. He is a terrific painter, and we have combined our specialties to be involved in a number of art shows. I am proud to say that I was recently named the Commemorative Artist of the Year at the Uptown Art Fair in Minneapolis. It was a great honor," says Matt.

Blair has also been heavily involved for many years in serving food at the Union Gospel Mission in St. Paul. "I first got involved in charity work as a rookie when Carl Eller approached me to do something with multiple sclerosis," recalls Matt. "Carl came up to me and said, 'You need to do this.' And I said back to him, 'Yes, sir, Mr. Eller, and I got involved.'

"Charity work is very important to me. I have been recently over in Haiti doing work. I want to help people. I know where I came from and how we had to struggle when I was growing up. It helped me to understand how important it is to do things for other people. I want to help out wherever I can and make a difference."

Blair will always be remembered for the great heart he showed on the football field. It seemed whenever a big play was needed in a game—a recovered fumble, a blocked kick, or an interception—Matt was there to come through in the clutch for the Vikings. He brought the crowds to their feet so many times in so many games. His lasting legacy will remain with Minnesota, both on the field and off.

5

In 1976, Blair was all over opponents, recovering a remarkable five fumbles in the season.

"He was outstanding against the run or pass and made many great plays."

—JERRY BURNS

"I have the highest regard for Matt as a person and as an athlete. He was a tremendous player who just seemed to get better and better as the years went by."

—JEFF SIEMON

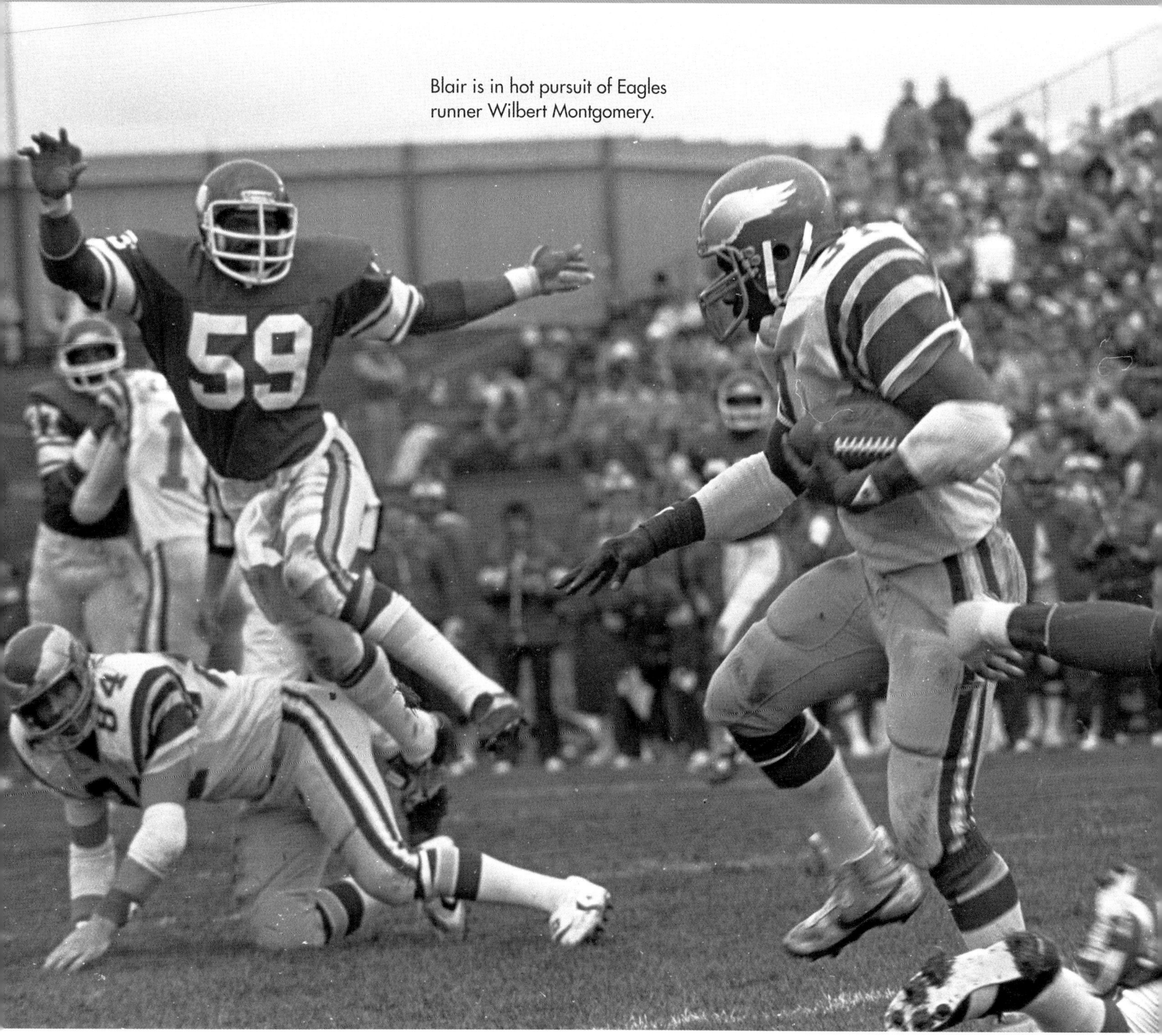

Blair is in hot pursuit of Eagles runner Wilbert Montgomery.

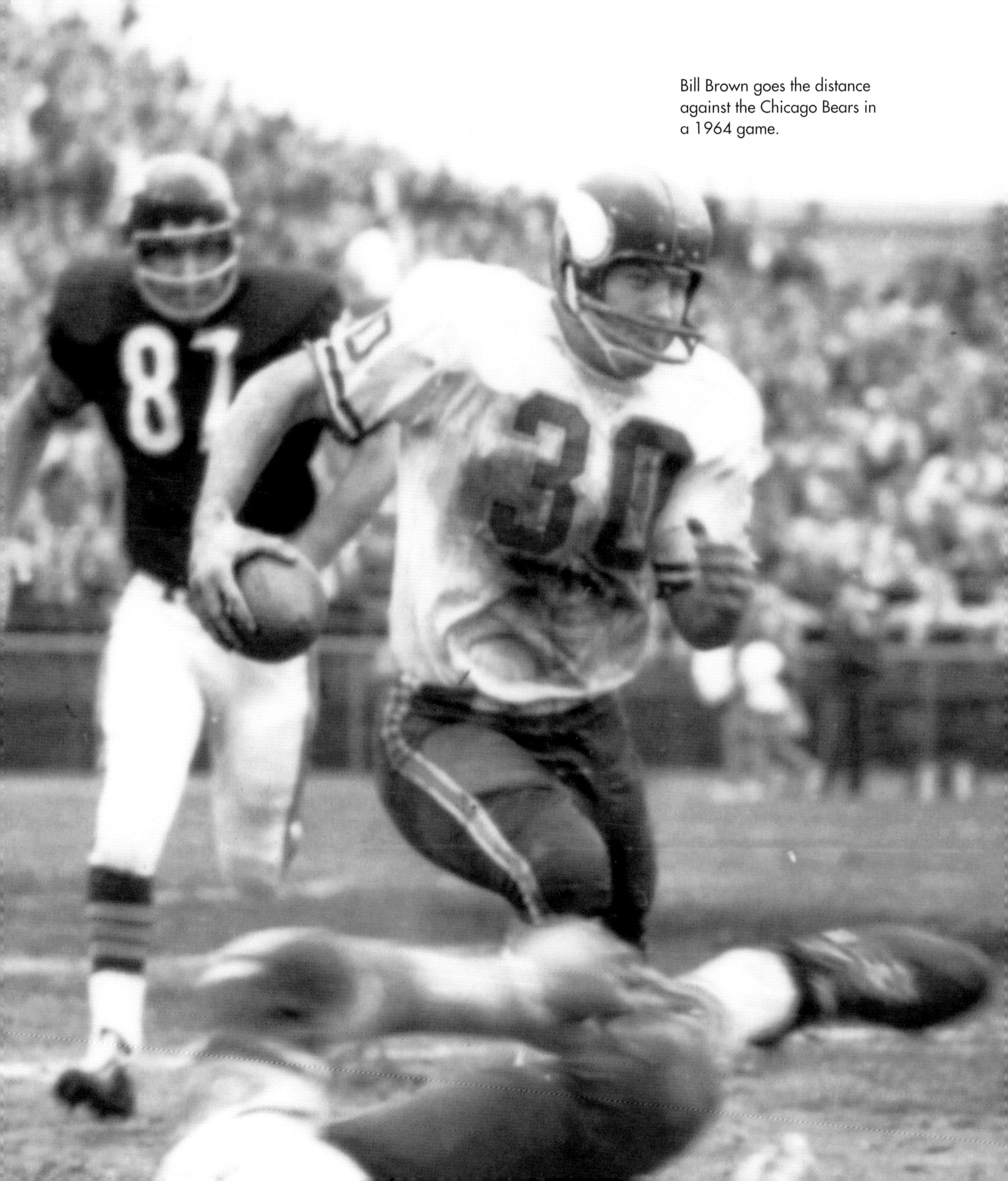

Bill Brown goes the distance against the Chicago Bears in a 1964 game.

Bill BROWN

#30 | Running Back, 1962–74

They called him Bill "Boom Boom" Brown, and he really fit the name. If you are fortunate to ever watch Bill sign his name, you will see him carefully write out BILL "BOOM BOOM" BROWN OLD NUMBER 30. To this day, he is a proud man. And if they measured toughness and love of the game as the primary criteria for All-Pro honors, Bill would have made the team every year that he played.

There may never be a player to wear the Purple as tough as Bill Brown was. His love for the game transformed into a fierce desire on the field to hit people. Hard.

A native of Mendota, Illinois, his interests always seemed to center around sports. While in high school, he excelled in football, basketball, and track. He was heavily recruited by many colleges, winning football scholarships to several Big Ten schools. He ultimately chose Illinois in order to remain somewhat close to home.

While at Illinois he was named All-Conference in the Big Ten and also won the shot-put title, setting a school record with a toss of 54 feet, 10.5 inches. His solid play as a tough, hard-nosed running fullback at Illinois got the attention of George Halas of the Chicago Bears in 1961, who drafted him in the second round.

After Brown spent the first year of his career in professional football with the Bears, Halas traded him to the Minnesota Vikings in 1962, in exchange for a fourth-round draft choice in the 1964 Draft. The Bears didn't think he could play; they were wrong. He played for 13 more years, running, blocking, and catching the football as well as anybody. He was named to the Pro Bowl following the 1964, 1965, 1967, and 1968 seasons and holds many Vikings records, including most games played by a running back (180) and career rushing attempts. He ranks fourth in career rushing yardage and is tied for second in career rushing touchdowns.

Former coach Jerry Burns has said that when he was coaching with the Green Bay Packers, legendary coach Vince Lombardi named only two NFL players on opposing rosters who had the ability to upset the Packers' game plan. One of them was Bill Brown.

Brown played the game with no concern for the abuse his body took. His coach for many years, Bud Grant, appreciated the player's passion and durability by rewarding him with the captain's role on special teams during his last year with the Vikings.

Hall of Fame Vikings quarterback Fran Tarkenton smiles when thinking of his former running back and the destruction he brought with him onto the playing field. "He played the game with an uncompromising toughness and

Brown scores against the rival Packers.

urgency," he says. "He absolutely loved every aspect of pro football. Bill Brown loved every second on the field, off the field, and in the locker room with his teammates. Bill was not only a terrific ball carrier but a bone-crushing blocker. And along with all this, he was as good a receiver as I have ever thrown the ball to. He was as pure a football player as there has ever been."

Although former general manger Mike Lynn was not one to personally socialize with players, Bill Brown was one of his absolute favorites. "One of my real sincere regrets when I was with the Vikings was not taking care of Bill

251

It was a banner year for Brown in 1966, when he led the league in rushing attempts—251, good for 829 yards.

High school senior portrait.
Photo courtesy of Bill Brown

Brown with his contract like I should have," recalls Lynn. "I should have given him more money. To this day, it still bothers me."

"I enjoyed every part of the game," says Brown. "And I loved playing for Bud Grant. Bud was a great person and a great football coach. It was all the wonderful friends that I made that makes me feel the best about the game," Brown continues. "I still see many of them quite often, like Mick Tingelhoff, Dave Osborn, and many others."

During the off-season while playing for the Vikings, Brown first worked with his father in the air-conditioning business. He later took up a second career working for the John Roberts Printing Company, where he worked for 25 years, finishing his career at Bromley Printing.

Today, Brown enjoys a quieter life. "I like to go to the senior center and play cribbage," says Brown. "I used to spend time out in the community doing signings and so forth but don't do that too much anymore, [though] it has always been fun to interact with the fans."

Brown is still often recognized and remembered. Thirteen years in Purple playing for the Minnesota Vikings cemented his legendary performances in the hearts and minds of the Vikings faithful. He will always be known for playing the game with a ferocity and passion rarely challenged.

Anyone who has ever had the opportunity to watch Bill Brown play the game of football will never forget him. It didn't matter if it was at practice, during the regular season, in the playoffs, or in the Super Bowl. He played with his heart, his soul, and every fiber in his body.

"I would play again if I could," he says. "I had a great time!"

"He was the best and the toughest. He could run, block, catch the ball, anything he was asked to do. He had a terrific attitude and was a tremendous football player."

—JERRY BURNS

Joey BROWNER

#47 | Defensive Back, 1983–91

If you ever saw a Minnesota Vikings football game when Joey Browner played the game, you saw someone special playing his heart out on the football field. And if you were in the stands and shut your eyes, you might have thought you were hearing a thunderstorm. That sound, however, was that of the bone-crushing tackles Browner laid on his opponents; he hit people like a runaway freight train! He was an all-around outstanding defensive player and a great tackler.

While playing for the Minnesota Vikings, he was selected to play in six Pro Bowls from 1985 to 1990, and his career with the Vikings lasted from 1983 to 1991.

His last year in professional football was spent playing for the Tampa Bay Buccaneers. Due to the hard-nosed approach and controlled fury that Browner brought to every single play, he also holds the proud distinction of being picked four times by former Oakland Raiders coach John Madden to the All-Madden Team. When you make the All-Madden Team, you are recognized as a standout player and, in addition, one who plays the game with more intensity, more ferocity, and more mayhem than the others. Joey Browner was unquestionably that kind of player.

Browner played his collegiate football at the University of Southern California, where he was a four-time All-American. As a youngster, he participated in a lot of group sports in his hometown, Warren, Ohio.

"I had my heroes to look up to," says Browner. "Great players like Paul Warfield and Willie Davenport and Oklahoma coach Bob Stoops were from our area. I watched sports on television some, programs like [*ABC's*] *Wide World of Sports*, and really enjoyed watching the Olympic Games. I loved to watch the track events, especially the runners."

Browner grew up with eight brothers and sisters. "After my father died in 1976, my mother moved us to Georgia to experience where my father grew up.... This was during my senior year in high school, and I got the opportunity to meet my father's side of the family. It was very hard to lose my father but great to meet his family," recalls Joey.

"It was an amazing time for me in my life. The Civil Rights Act was only 10 years old, and I got to experience what it was like in the South. The changes, for the most part, at that particular time were smaller than a mustard seed, and it really opened my eyes to the world," he recalls. "I grew up and worked hard in school. I told my mom that I would always keep our name in a positive light."

Joey wasn't the only member of the Browner family who excelled in sports. In fact, the Browner family has had more

Browner clobbers the Rams' Eric Dickerson during game play.

players in the National Football League than any other. His brother Ross played for the Cincinnati Bengals and the Green Bay Packers; brother Jimmy was also with the Bengals; brother Keith played with Tampa Bay, San Diego, San Francisco, and Los Angeles; nephew Max played with the Steelers; and Joey played with the Vikings and Tampa Bay.

He was an All-State defensive lineman in Ohio as a junior and also played basketball and ran track and field. After his senior year in Georgia, he earned *Parade* All-American honors and was named Atlanta-Area Player of the Year.

Browner was recruited by schools across the country, ending up at the University of Southern California. In 1982 he was voted the Most Valuable Player at USC. A terrific defensive back for the Trojans, he shared the backfield with future Tennessee Titans coach Jeff Fisher and soon-to-be San Francisco 49ers great Ronnie Lott. During his outstanding career in college football, Joey also played with Hall of Fame tackle Anthony Muñoz and running backs Marcus Allen and Charles White. He recorded a phenomenal 243 tackles at USC and played in the Rose Bowl and Fiesta Bowl.

In August 2009, Browner started the Joey Browner Foundation as a part of his ongoing contributions to the community. (Previously he had worked diligently as a coordinator of the Olympic Games for Native American people.) With his foundation, Joey has realized his dream of assisting young people in need. His involvement has been a continuing source of inspiration.

"It's what keeps me going," says Browner. "I need to get up every morning and feel like I am making a difference in people's lives, especially those of our children. I need to find a way to stand up for those who cannot stand up for themselves."

Browner has very strong feelings about preparing youth for the future and does it through his foundation. The organization strives to promote both physical activity and education as intertwined goals for young people, while also promoting a strong component of community involvement for youth. Browner's foundation begins with prekindergarten-age kids, setting a strong foundation for future successes. Leadership, he believes, is a skill that cannot be learned early enough. He has been a true role model.

Browner was a leader on the field.

1

Browner ranked first in the league in fumble returns for touchdowns in 1984 and interceptions returned for touchdowns in 1985.

"Joey Browner is a great guy and a remarkable athlete. He may have been the most physically gifted defensive back to ever play for the Vikings."

—SCOTT STUDWELL

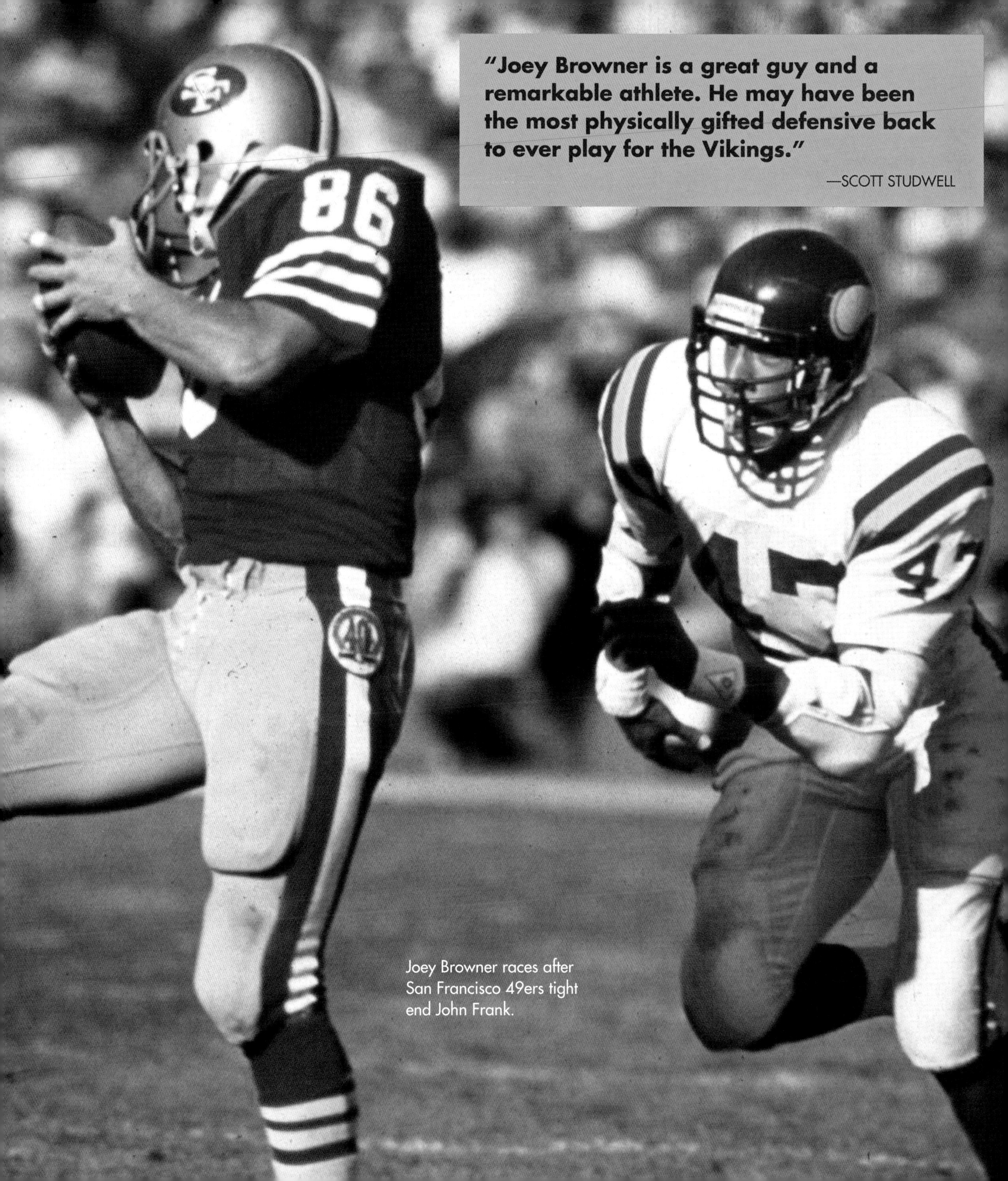

Joey Browner races after San Francisco 49ers tight end John Frank.

Bobby Bryant wrestles down a Packers ball carrier during game action.

Bobby BRYANT

#20 | Cornerback, 1968–80

Bobby Bryant grew up in Macon, Georgia, one of 11 children—five boys and six girls. "We all played sports and loved every minute of it," remembers Bobby. "We were basically a poor family. My dad was a carpenter and worked hard to put food on the table for all of us. My mom was a hard worker also. We were a strong Christian family and went to church every Sunday."

Bobby began his involvement in organized sports starting in the fourth grade. He played football, basketball, baseball, and ran track, and he excelled at each. "I was always the smallest kid on the team, but I had really good speed, so I was able to play well," he continues.

"Playing well" was perhaps an understatement. Bryant earned 21 letters playing on his high school teams. He was recruited by several college teams, mostly from small colleges. He settled on the University of South Carolina as a 6'0", 140-pound halfback and defensive back. Since freshmen were not eligible at the time, Bobby had to wait until his sophomore year to start, while also returning kicks for South Carolina.

He began his collegiate career as a two-sport athlete in football and as a sprinter and hurdler in track. In the spring of his freshman year, Bobby went out for baseball and became a superior left-handed pitcher for the Gamecocks. Bryant started the next four years in football and baseball and was a First-Team All-Atlantic Coast Conference selection his senior year in both baseball and football.

In baseball, his arm prowess led him to strike out 100 batters in a season, and he once pitched and completed a 13-inning game against Maryland. He was drafted by the New York Yankees in 1966 and the Boston Red Sox after his senior season the following year.

Bobby won the Anthony J. McKelvin Award, which is given annually to the conference's outstanding athlete. He was named to several All-American football teams and played in the Hula Bowl and the East-West Shrine Game. He was well known in college for some unbelievable punt returns, including one for a record 98 yards in a game against North Carolina State. He was elected to the University of South Carolina Athletic Hall of Fame and also the State of South Carolina Athletic Hall of Fame.

"I always felt that I could play," recalls Bobby. "But I never played very much until my junior year at South Carolina. I was very surprised when I got drafted by the Minnesota Vikings in the seventh round of the 1967 NFL Draft."

During Bryant's senior season, he hurt his knee. Unfortunately, the injury followed him to the professional

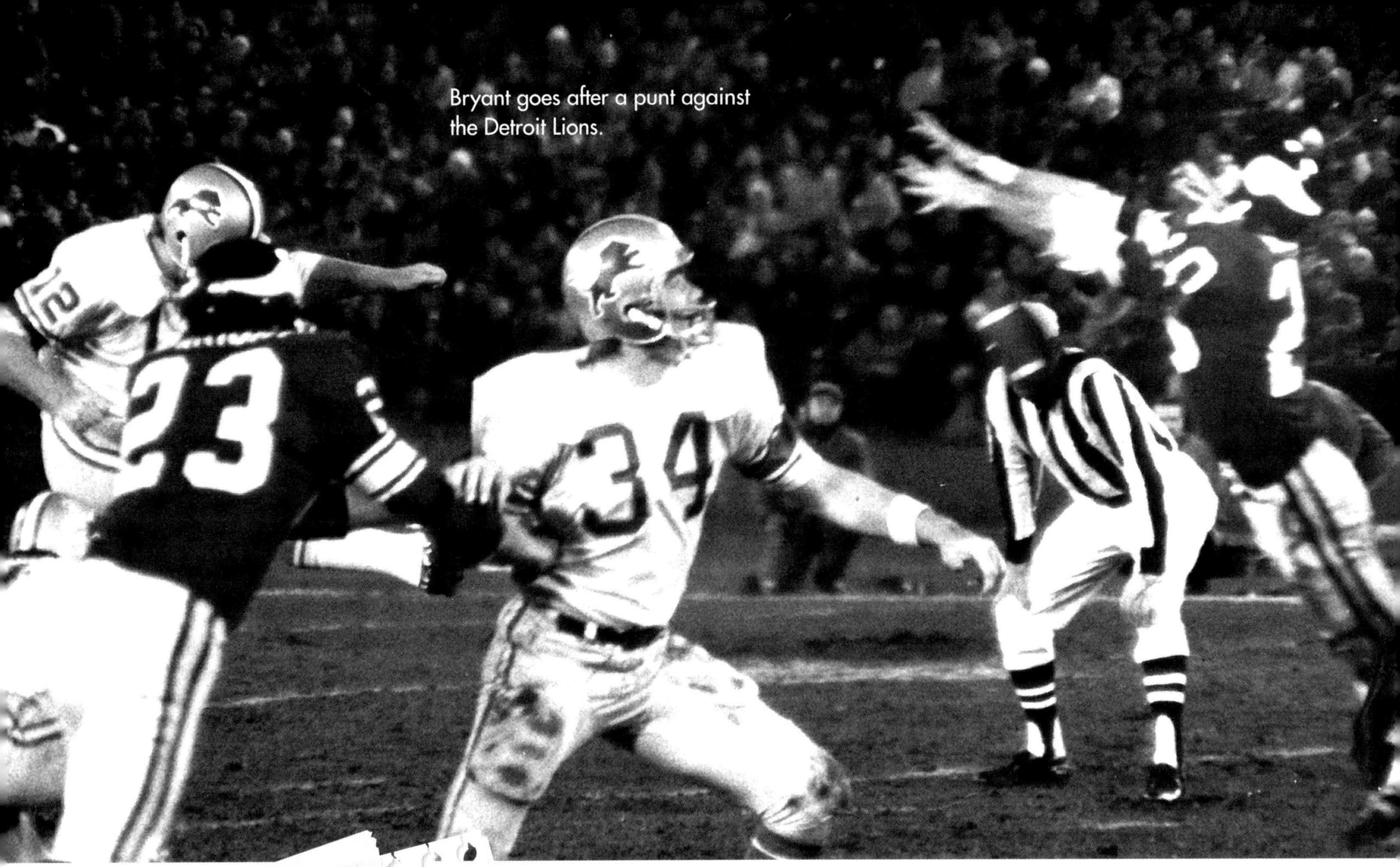

Bryant goes after a punt against the Detroit Lions.

football ranks and kept him out of the game during his first season in Minnesota.

"I was only able to get a little action my first year in pro ball," recalls Bryant. "I got to play in one exhibition game, hurt my knee again, and sat out the rest of the season."

It didn't take long after that first year, however, for Bryant to come on as a strong player in the defensive backfield for the Vikings. Early on, he intercepted a pass and proved he was going to be a strong player for years to come in Minnesota. By 1969, he had become a regular player and remained so for more than a decade. All in all, he played in the National Football League for 14 seasons, longer than any other former University of South Carolina player in history.

During the off-season, Bobby worked at Northwestern National Bank as a bond salesman. He did that for two

8

Bryant ranked No. 2 in the league in 1969, when he made eight interceptions in the season.

years, and then he and former Vikings defensive back Charlie West opened up a clothing store in the Twin Cities called One Leg Up. "This didn't turn out very well for us," he recalls. "We only kept the shop open for about two years.

"I had to find something else to do, so I ended up buying the rights to the Vikings traveling basketball team from [my] former teammate Karl Kasulke. He took over ownership of the off-season team and set up all the bookings and game arrangements.

"We had quite a team," says Bryant. "We had Bob Lurtsema, Alan Page, Clinton Jones, Charlie West, Matt Blair, Doug Sutherland, Ed White, and others. We played in small towns against local teams all over the state and region. And we won most of our games."

Five years later, he sold the team to Lurtsema. Eventually Bobby's love of the South called him back, and he returned to his friends, family, and warm weather.

Outside of the work arena, Bobby has had a special interest in softball and has participated on many tournament teams over the years. He enjoys playing golf and still has a connection to the Twin Cities (his daughter lives in the area).

Bobby Bryant was a solid big-play defensive back, who netted a career total of 51 interceptions in his years with the Vikings and made it to Pro Bowls following the 1975 and 1976 seasons.

"When I looked at the roster of possibilities for the 50 greatest players, I never thought I would have a chance to make the team. It was and still is a very special feeling," he says of the honor.

For the fans who watched Bryant play the game, it was a given—too many seasons, too many great plays.

Bryant intercepts a pass against the St. Louis Cardinals.

"Bobby Bryant made more big game plays than anyone on our team."

—FRAN TARKENTON

Anthony CARTER

#81 | Wide Receiver, 1985–93

Anthony Carter was one of the few athletes in professional sports who had the big-play ability to literally take over a game. In 1987, in a playoff game against the San Francisco 49ers, he did just that. Carter had 10 receptions for a then-playoff record 227 yards in the Vikings' 36–24 upset of the 49ers. During those 1987 playoffs, he recorded an incredible 642 all-purpose yards for an NFL postseason record.

Growing up in Riviera Beach, Florida, football was the furthest thing from Anthony's mind. "I wanted to be a firefighter," says Carter. "As a young person, I was always very quiet, and even today I don't care for a lot of attention," says Anthony. "I worked hard as a youngster. I worked as a bag boy in a local grocery store and always gave my best at things I did.

"I was a big Miami Dolphins fan as a kid, but I never gave football much thought at all for college or as a career," he continues. Anthony grew up the youngest of five brothers in his family, which included seven sisters as well. He attended high school at Suncoast High in Riviera Beach and excelled at football, basketball, and track. He was called "the Little Gnat" because of his size and speed—he was a star performer in high school at a mere 155 pounds.

He was heavily recruited in the South but ended up going to Michigan—where he became one of the best to ever wear a Wolverines uniform. He shocked fans, coaches, and fellow players with his exploits on the field. The first time he ever touched the football in a game, as a ninth-grader at Suncoast High School, he returned a kickoff 87 yards for a touchdown. The same thing happened at Michigan, except this time it was a punt—he returned it 78 yards for a touchdown.

Carter won three-time All-American honors at Michigan during his career from 1979 to 1982. He set records that will likely never be broken. He was practically unstoppable, completing uncatchable catches and turning them into more yards after completion. He earned the distinction of being named the Most Valuable Player in the Big Ten Conference in 1982, the Most Valuable Player at the University of Michigan in 1980 and 1982, and All–Big Ten Conference in 1980, 1981, and 1982. He was consistently in the running for the Heisman Trophy, finishing in the top 10 three different times. He was elected to the College Football Hall of Fame in 2001.

His numbers and overall statistics at Michigan were groundbreaking. In his collegiate career, he had 36 touchdowns and 240 points. This broke the point totals of the great Tommy Harmon, who starred at Michigan from 1938 to 1940. During Anthony's years with the Wolverines,

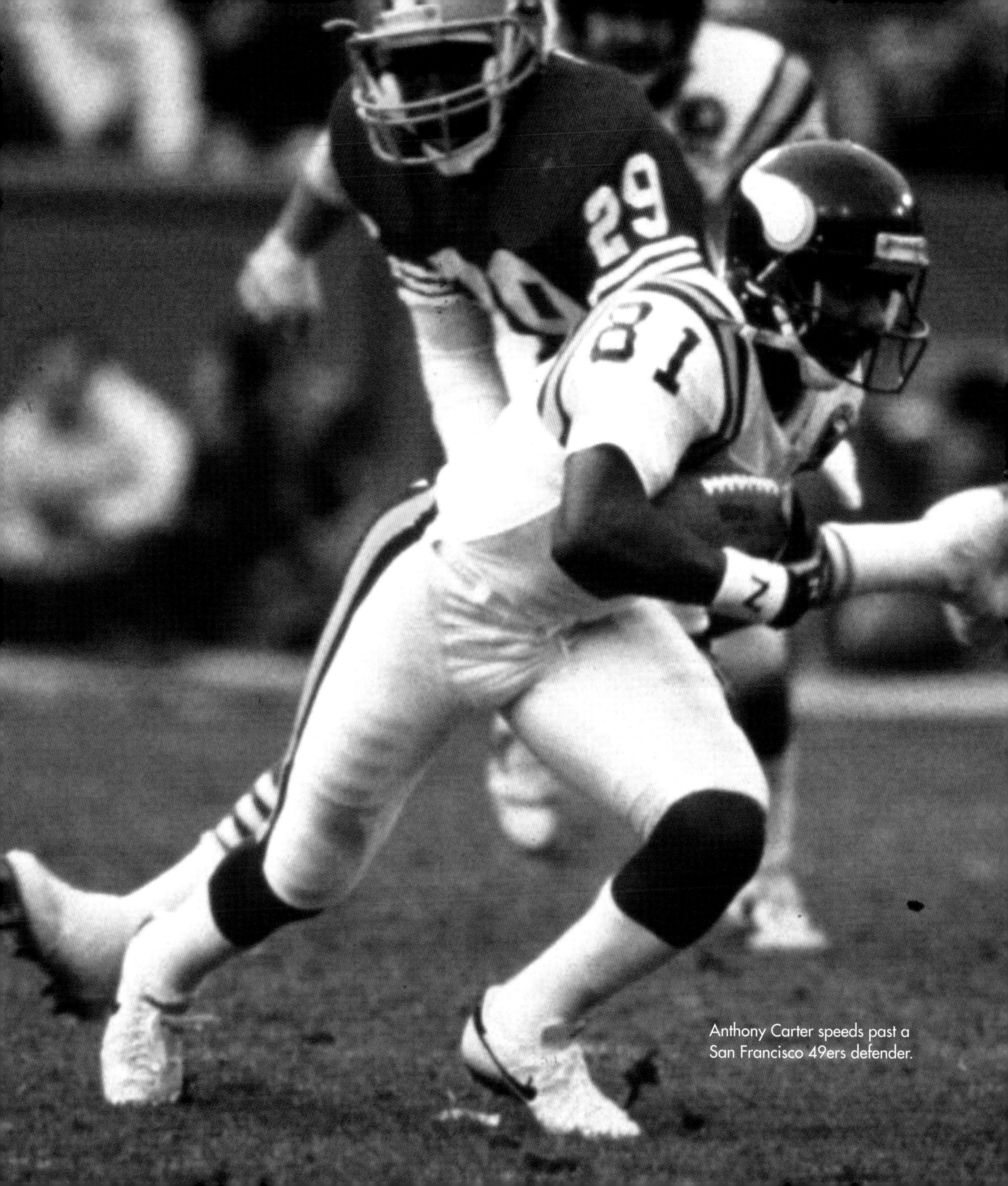

Anthony Carter speeds past a San Francisco 49ers defender.

they won two Big Ten Championships, played in four bowl games, and won the Rose Bowl and the Bluebonnet Bowl.

Upon graduation, Carter held practically every receiving and return record at Michigan. He had become the all-time leader in touchdowns (40), receiving passes (161), receiving yardage (3,076), touchdown pass receptions (37), punt returns (79), punt-return yardage (907), kickoff returns (63), and kickoff yardage (1,606). Some of these records still stand today.

After his eligibility was up at Michigan, Carter was drafted by the Miami Dolphins but signed with the newly formed United States Football League's Michigan Panthers. He played for two seasons with the Panthers, having stalwart seasons.

Before the 1985 campaign, the Panthers merged with the Oakland Invaders; it was to be his last season in the USFL. Following the season, he signed with the Miami Dolphins and was subsequently traded to the Minnesota Vikings.

Carter quickly became a dominant force on his new team. During the first six years in Minnesota, he led the team in receptions five of his first six seasons. He was selected to the Pro Bowl each year from 1987 to 1989 and was a two-time Second-Team All-NFC selection in 1987 and 1988. All in all, he was a spectacular player for Minnesota from 1985 to 1993.

He finished his NFL career back where it began in college—Michigan—by joining the Detroit Lions. Unfortunately, it ended with two injury-plagued seasons.

In his 11 seasons in the National Football League, Carter totaled 486 receptions and 55 touchdowns. His records and play were nothing short of phenomenal. But if you compare it to the way Anthony Carter lives his life today, it would have to take a backseat. Anthony Carter now lives for his son, Anthony Carter Jr., who has cerebral palsy. He was born with the disease, and it has left him in a wheelchair. Carter's devotion to his son and to the disease is incredible and worthy of the highest esteem.

Carter Sr. could be involved today in just about anything he would choose in the working world. Instead, he

24.3

Proof positive that he was a key to the Vikings' potent offensive attack, Carter led the NFL in 1987 with a robust 24.3-yards-per-catch average.

focuses his attention on fund-raising for cerebral palsy research and spending time with his son. "He is 16 years old now and a great kid," says the proud father. "I would prefer spending as much time as I can with him."

Keeping himself out of the spotlight was a big job for Anthony Carter, but he has always preferred to eschew the attention. He has always been that way. Even after being selected as a member of the 50 greatest Vikings team, Carter deflected attention from himself. "It means a lot to me to be recognized as one of the 50 greatest Vikings of all time. I was fortunate to play on some great teams with some great players."

"Anthony was a teammate that you would go to war with. He never left anything on the field. When that ball went into the air, he would go after it and catch it at the top of his jump."

—TIM IRWIN

Carter shows off his receiving form in this snapshot. *Photo courtesy of Anthony Carter*

Minnesota Vikings Ring of Honor Members (Date of Induction)

Fran Tarkenton (September 9, 1998)
Alan Page (September 20, 1998)
Jim Finks (October 18, 1998)
Bud Grant (November 8, 1998)
Paul Krause (November 15, 1998)
Fred Zamberletti (December 20, 1998)
Jim Marshall (November 28, 1999)
Ron Yary (September 9, 2001)
Korey Stringer (November 19, 2001)
Mick Tingelhoff (November 25, 2001)
Carl Eller (November 10, 2002)
Cris Carter (September 14, 2003)
Bill Brown (September 26, 2004)
Jerry Burns (November 6, 2005)
Randall McDaniel (December 17, 2006)
Chuck Foreman (September 30, 2007)
John Randle (November 30, 2008)
Scott Studwell (November 29, 2009)
Chris Doleman (October 23, 2011)

Chuck Foreman

Pro Football Hall of Fame Inductees (Date of Induction)

Fran Tarkenton (August 2, 1986)
Alan Page (July 30, 1988)
Bud Grant (July 30, 1994)
Jim Finks (July 29, 1995)
Paul Krause (July 1, 1998)
Ron Yary (August 4, 2001)
Carl Eller (August 8, 2004)
Gary Zimmerman (August 2, 2008)
Randall McDaniel (August 8, 2009)
John Randle (August 7, 2010)
Chris Doleman (August 4, 2012)

Fran Tarkenton and Bud Grant

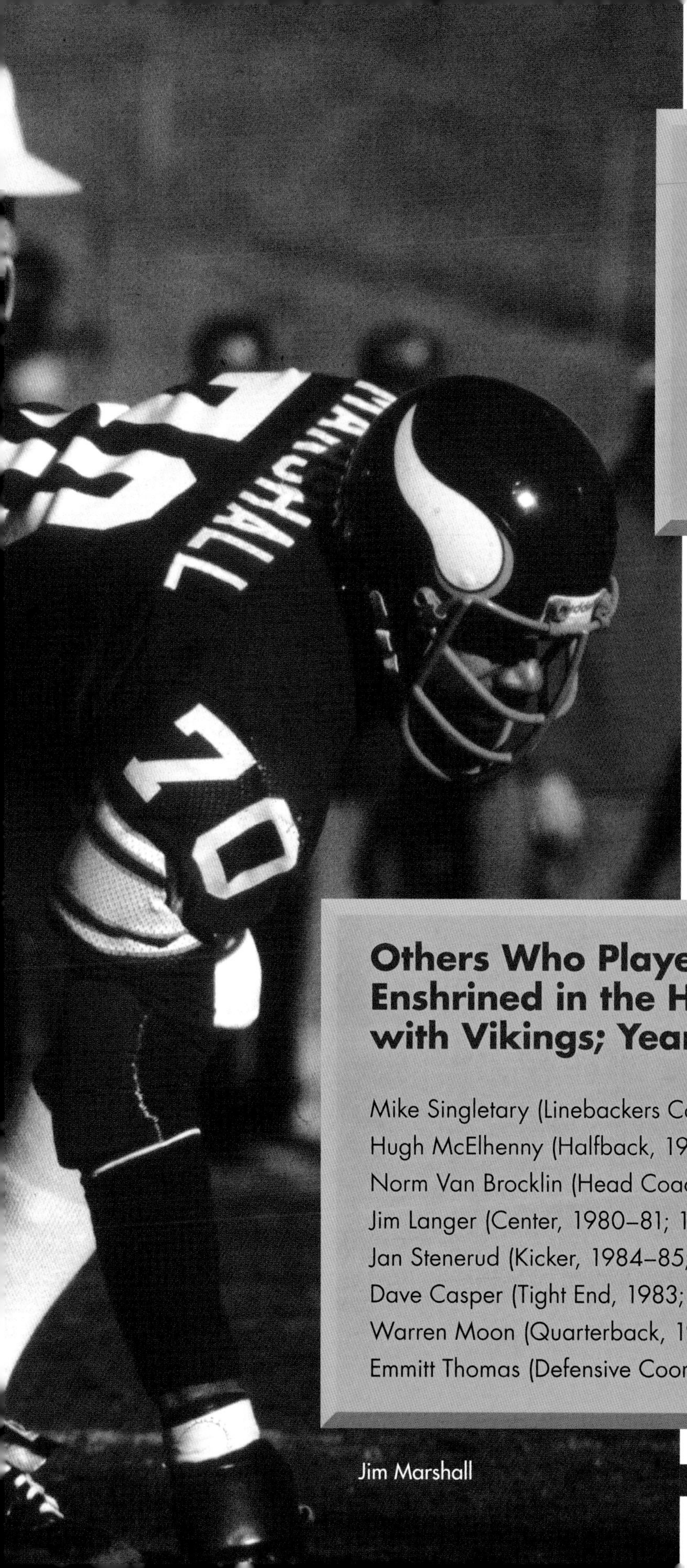

Jim Marshall

Retired Jersey Numbers (Date of Retirement)

#10 – Fran Tarkenton (October 7, 1979)
#88 – Alan Page (September 25, 1988)
#70 – Jim Marshall (November 28, 1999)
#77 – Korey Stringer (November 19, 2001)
#53 – Mick Tingelhoff (November 25, 2001)
#80 – Cris Carter (September 14, 2003)

Norm Van Brocklin

Others Who Played or Coached for the Vikings Enshrined in the Hall of Fame (Position, Tenure with Vikings; Year of Induction)

Mike Singletary (Linebackers Coach, Special Assistant to Head Coach, 2011; 1998)
Hugh McElhenny (Halfback, 1961–62; 1970)
Norm Van Brocklin (Head Coach, 1961–66; 1971)
Jim Langer (Center, 1980–81; 1987)
Jan Stenerud (Kicker, 1984–85; 1991)
Dave Casper (Tight End, 1983; 2002)
Warren Moon (Quarterback, 1994–96; 2006)
Emmitt Thomas (Defensive Coordinator, 2000–01; 2008)

Cris Carter celebrates six.

"He may have been the best sideline receiver who ever played the game."

—JERRY BURNS

Cris CARTER

#80 | Wide Receiver, 1990–2001

Cris Carter's inclusion among the 50 greatest Vikings was not a head-scratcher, by any stretch of the imagination. He is without question one of the greatest wide receivers to ever play the game of professional football. He is on the doorstep to the Pro Football Hall of Fame and will someday enter its elite ranks.

During his 12-year career in the National Football League, Carter was a dominant receiver who spent a lot of time in possession of the football in opponents' end zones. He ranks eighth all-time in touchdowns scored, with 131, and fourth in receiving touchdowns, with 130. His total yards of 13,899 in receiving ranks eighth in the NFL record books. He led the National Football League in receiving touchdowns three times and had eight consecutive seasons of at least 78 catches.

Although his history was soundly built as a member of the Minnesota Vikings, Cris began his career with the Philadelphia Eagles in 1987, where he spent three years before being traded to Minnesota. He finished his career in Miami during the 2002 season.

Carter was born in Troy, Ohio. He first played organized football when he was eight years old. He excelled at both sports immediately and was known for his extreme competitive spirit, even as a youngster. He desperately wanted to win. "As a youngster, I loved sports, and it was really all that I was interested in," recalls Cris. "I loved playing football and basketball and had set my sights on playing professional basketball, which was my favorite of the two sports."

He spent his early years living in Middleton, Ohio, in a small housing-project apartment with his mother and five siblings. At Middleton High School, Cris was an outstanding athlete in both football and basketball, leading to a career at Ohio State.

"I was originally going to play basketball and football at Ohio State," says Carter, "but after an injury in the Rose Bowl game, I decided to concentrate on football…and also because I thought I could make the biggest difference playing wide receiver in professional football."

His timing, route running, and ability to make spectacular leaping catches soon elevated him to one of the best college receivers in the nation. He once completed a catch that was designed to be a "throwaway" out of bounds by the Buckeyes quarterback. He signed with an agent instead of going on to a senior-year season at OSU, but even without that final year, he left with the Ohio State record for receptions at 168. In 2000, he was named to the Ohio State All-Century Team.

Carter poses with local schoolchildren during a visit in 2000.

"I could have gone to just about any college after high school," says Cris. "I was heavily recruited from all over, but it was really important to my mom that I go to Ohio State, so that's where I went."

Carter was selected by the Philadelphia Eagles in the fourth round of the NFL Supplemental Draft in 1987, but he saw little action in his first season in the NFL. In 1990, he was picked up by the Minnesota Vikings. The 1991 season was his breakout year, when he finished with a total of 72 pass receptions for 962 yards.

As a member of the Minnesota Vikings, Carter was outstanding. He was extremely adept at keeping possession of the football and may have been one of the best sideline receivers to have ever played the game. He caught passes all over the football field, and teammates counted on him in big-game, big-play situations. He delivered. He had tremendous instincts for the game and incredible hands. He also understood the game and its intricacies. He left the Vikings in 2001 after amassing a staggering 1,004 receptions for 12,383 total yards and 110 touchdowns.

Carter has found many successes off the field as well. While with the Minnesota Vikings, he was extremely active in the community. He developed a program called the Viking Super Challenge, for which he and teammates adopted schools in the Minneapolis area. The goal was to offer support and guidance to the students, promoting individual responsibility and accountability. It was very crucial to him that players participate with schools that were similar to those from their own past experiences.

"We challenged the kids, over a period of years, to stay away from premarital sex, alcohol, drugs," says Carter. "We kept regular contact with the kids over a long period of time, and I believe we made a difference. It was a terrific program."

The development and implementation of this program earned Carter the Walter Payton Man of the Year Award in 1999. He was also the recipient of the Bart Starr Man of the Year Award for his leadership on the field, in the home, and in the community in 1995. In 1998, he won the Byron

"Whizzer" White Award as the NFL Man of the Year for his contributions in the community.

"I'm still very active in the community," says Carter. "I do a lot of faith-type activities and coach high school football in south Florida. I love working with the young wide receivers. My greatest passion, though, is spending time with my wife and kids."

Cris now works as a broadcast journalist for ESPN and also serves Yahoo Sports as a football analyst.

"It has been a great career after football," he reflects. "It is something I thought about doing for a long time, and I have really enjoyed [staying] active with the game."

For those who have been enamored with the Purple over the decades, how can one ever forget the incredible accomplishments that Carter made for the Minnesota Vikings? His uncanny ability to make spectacular catches and steady game-day contributions has given fans the opportunity to enjoy his attributes for many seasons.

"I really enjoyed my time with the Vikings," says Carter. "They were great years on and off the field. I grew up a lot as a person and believe I was able to make a significant impact in the community. It was a tremendous honor to be named one of the 50 greatest Vikings. There were so many great players who played in Minnesota, and I am grateful that I was included."

3

No one can deny what a threat Carter was on the football field. He topped the NFL in receiving touchdowns in three different seasons.

Carter sets his sights on the end zone.

Fred COX

#14 | Kicker, 1963–77

Fred Cox is the all-time leading scorer for the Vikings with 1,365 points, which includes 282 field goals. He played with the Minnesota Vikings for 15 seasons after being drafted by the Cleveland Browns in the eighth round of the 1961 National Football League Player Draft. During his long career with Minnesota, he became one of 10 Vikings with the distinction of playing in all of the team's four Super Bowls.

Cox was an extremely accurate kicker who led the NFL in scoring in 1969 and again in 1970, with 121 and 125 points respectively. In addition to being the team's place-kicker, Cox also was the Vikings' punter in his rookie season with the team.

He played college football at the University of Pittsburgh and was drafted in 1961 as a running back by both the Browns and the New York Titans of the American Football League. A gifted athlete, Cox handled the kicking duties for the Vikings for more than a decade but also helped out the team in many other on-field capacities during practices.

"I grew up in the mining and mill area of Pennsylvania. My uncles all worked in the mines, and my family ran a local grocery store. After over 60 years now, the family still owns the store in Monongahela, Pennsylvania," says Cox.

"I went to Pillsbury High School and played football, basketball, baseball, and soccer," he continues. "I loved to hunt and fish, so that occupied a lot of my spare time growing up. We did a lot of deer hunting up in the mountains and quite a bit of pheasant hunting also. Still, to this day, we do a lot of family hunting together…

"After high school, I pretty much had my choice of where I wanted to go to school. There was some interest

> **"I am one day younger than Fred, [and] I always enjoyed telling him how old he looked! Fred was a great contributor to the team. He was always there to help out in any way he could on and off the field."**
>
> —GRADY ALDERMAN

Fred Cox launches one through the uprights.

"Fred was one of the last of the straight-on kickers. He was very accurate, scored a lot of points, and made some big kicks for us. He was with the Vikings for a long time."

—JERRY BURNS

[from] the Pittsburgh Pirates for baseball, but I didn't see that making much sense, so I stayed with football."

At the University of Pittsburgh, Cox played both offense and defense as a running back and defensive back. He also did the kicking. When the Cleveland Browns drafted Cox, they selected him hoping he would be the blocking back for the great Jim Brown. Little attention was given at the time to his kicking prowess, because the Browns had the great Lou Groza on their roster. In fact, Cox hadn't kicked a field goal at Pittsburgh until his senior year—then he hit highlight reel–caliber shots with field goals of 45 and 52 yards in a single game against the Fighting Irish of Notre Dame.

The Browns actually drafted Cox a year before his senior year because he had been redshirted one season; he eventually went to the Browns after his eligibility expired. Cox suffered a back injury in Cleveland, which also limited his duties to kicking for the Browns. "They had Lou, 'the Toe' Groza, and they weren't about to let him go," Cox recalls. "But I will say this about Groza: he taught me more about kicking than any person I have ever known."

In 1962, the Browns traded Cox to Minnesota, where he had an outstanding training camp—but still suffered the fate of being cut from the team. The next year he was brought back and made the team; he remained for the next 15 years.

"We had a great group of players in Minnesota," Cox says. "We not only played football together, but we did other things together also. Many of us liked to hunt, and we spent a lot of time with each other. Players like Dave Osborn, Mick Tingelhoff, Wally Hilgenberg, Fran

1,365

Cox's 1,365 career points for the Vikings give him a "leg up" on the rest of the competition, making him the franchise's all-time leading scorer.

Cox stands beside some of his cherished memorabilia.
Photo courtesy of Fred Cox

Tarkenton, and so many others were great teammates and great guys," recalls Cox.

The back injury that plagued Cox after he signed with the Browns gave him a taste of what he wanted to do in life beyond the football field. "Because of some of the chiropractic work done for me [I was inspired] to take up this trade," he says. During the off-season he went to chiropractic school, graduating in 1972. He opened his own practice in 1975, and in the first year in his new profession, he made *twice* the money he did his last year of playing professional football. He stayed in the profession for 20 years.

"One day a man came to my door and provided what I like to call an 'instant retirement.' I thought he wanted me to invest in something, and I told him that I wasn't interested. What he wanted was just some advice on a portable goalpost to be moved around from yard to yard for kids to kick the ball over. From there, we talked about the kind of football that could be used. As a result, the Nerf football was invented by us." The invention, as we all know, was a blockbuster.

"After close to 40 years, the Nerf football is still a popular item," Cox continues. "A few years ago, over eight million were sold.... It was a great knock on my door."

Cox has suffered some health problems through the years but has remained upbeat and strong-willed. "I like to help other people," he says. "If I can help someone out to be successful, then I really want to do that. My goal in life is to help anyone I can to succeed," says Cox.

"When I was named to the 50 greatest Vikings list, it was really special for me. I am extremely proud of the honor. I really appreciate the Wilf family and how they have embraced the legacy of the Vikings alumni. They are great owners. They treat us older players so well. Zygi Wilf took the time to call me personally when I was asked recently to blow the Viking Horn before the game. It was a great honor for me."

Fred Cox is now fully retired and enjoying life. The memories of his years with the Vikings and the many friendships that he made stand out for him as being very special. "I lived the dream life," he says.

He came to the Vikings in 1963 as an unproven kicker; he left some 15 years later as the team's all-time leading scorer. He was consistent and he was one of the best ever.

"If I had one field goal or extra point that was needed to win a football game, I would want Fred Cox kicking it," Fran Tarkenton says. His reliability and scoring superlatives are just two of the reasons why Fred Cox is one of the chosen 50.

Culpepper zones in on a receiver during a matchup against the Saints on December 15, 2002.

Daunte CULPEPPER

#11 | Quarterback, 1999–2005

Daunte Culpepper had it all. He could run, throw, and hit people like a ton of bricks when scrambling for a first down. He was a model quarterback with all the credentials to be a team's franchise leader for a decade or more. But somehow, for some reason, it never worked out that way.

Culpepper was born in Ocala, Florida; his mother was in prison at the time of his birth. When he was one day old, he was adopted by Emma Lewis Culpepper and raised with more than 15 other children in Ocala.

Attending Vanguard High School, Daunte excelled in football, basketball, and baseball. His high school accomplishments on the Florida gridiron are legendary, and Culpepper achieved great honors by winning the Mr. Football Award from the state of Florida following his senior season in 1994. In 2007, he was named to the FHSAA's All-Century Team, which named the 33 top players in the history of Florida football during its 100 years of competition.

Culpepper was heavily recruited by colleges and ended up at the University of Central Florida. Despite great success in baseball at the high school level, he concentrated his attention on the football field at UCF. He wasted no time, shattering numerous school records at quarterback. He threw for more than 10,000 yards—a staggering mark for a collegiate athlete. He also set a national NCAA passing mark when he completed a record 73.6 percent of his throws, surpassing the former mark set by NFL great Steve Young. Young had held the mark for more than 15 years. Culpepper held on to the record until 2008.

But passing wasn't Culpepper's only recognized skill as a football player. He was also an outstanding runner and rushed for more than 1,000 yards in his collegiate career. While at Central Florida, he finished his astounding career with 12,459 total yards and 108 touchdowns (84 of them passing and 24 rushing).

Coming out of college, Culpepper was high on the draft boards of many NFL teams as they prepared for the 1999 NFL Draft. He lasted only to the 11th pick of the first round, when he was selected by the Minnesota Vikings. After absorbing the role as a backup to the quarterback position in his first year in the league, Culpepper was named the starting quarterback for the Vikings for the 2000 season. He led the team to wins in the first seven games.

The Vikings were not so successful in the remainder of the season, but they still made it to the NFC Championship Game, only to be defeated soundly by the New York Giants. Although the loss to New York was tough to swallow, Culpepper had an outstanding first year in the NFL to be

Culpepper is all smiles at a community event.

In 2003, Culpepper and the Vikings rebounded, improving their record to nine wins and seven losses. Unfortunately, it wasn't enough to make the playoffs.

Even so, it was a great year for the now-veteran signal caller, and he was rewarded with his second trip to the Pro Bowl.

By the beginning of the 2004 campaign, Culpepper had established himself in the league as a top-flight quarterback with a great arm and running skills that made anyone in his way pay a huge price for trying to tackle him. He was big, strong, and possessed a tremendous desire to punish anyone in his path.

The team stalled to 8–8 in 2004, but Culpepper was phenomenal. He passed for more than 4,700 yards and threw 39 touchdown passes with only 11 interceptions—good for a third Pro Bowl selection. He also set an NFL record for combined rushing and passing with 5,123 yards.

proud of, throwing for 33 touchdowns and passing for just below 4,000 total yards.

Teaming up with outstanding wide receiver Randy Moss, the two formed a dangerous combination. Culpepper was selected at the end of the season to play in his first Pro Bowl game. It looked as though Minnesota had found its franchise quarterback; better days were ahead.

Unfortunately, life in the NFL as a quarterback is not always filled with success, and each season brings differences and new challenges. Culpepper was not as proficient in his next two seasons with the Vikings, and he failed to play out the full season in 2001 after suffering a serious knee injury.

The following year, 2002, remained difficult for Daunte, who suffered some passing-proficiency difficulties. However, he really excelled at running the football and achieved the top mark for rushing touchdowns among NFL quarterbacks with 10.

Culpepper had become an established NFL quarterback and a star performer. He was a dangerous threat both throwing and running the football. Then in the seventh game of the 2005 season, Culpepper was severely injured in a game against the Carolina Panthers. He was placed on injured reserve by the Vikings after doctors found damage in four of the major knee ligaments.

In 2006, Daunte planned a return from his knee injury and began contract negotiations with the Vikings and the new team owners. The Vikings wanted Daunte to rehab his injured knee in Minnesota, but Culpepper refused and worked on his rehab in his home state of Florida. Furthermore, Culpepper and new head coach Brad Childress also did not mesh. It eventually led to a parting of the ways for Culpepper and the team.

The Vikings traded Culpepper to the Miami Dolphins for a second-round draft pick. His time in Miami did not go well. Continuing problems with his knee, as well as shoulder difficulties and management issues, led to his release before the 2007 season.

In midsummer of 2007, Culpepper was signed by the Oakland Raiders. He started only six games for Oakland before a hamstring injury ended yet another season. Shortly before the start of the 2008 season, Daunte Culpepper announced his retirement from professional football after being unsuccessful in obtaining a satisfactory contract from another team. It didn't take long, however, before he was back in the fold, signing with the Detroit Lions. He played in only four games with Detroit in 2008 before suffering yet another crippling injury, this time to his shoulder.

The Lions kept Culpepper under contract to start the 2009 season, but another injury to his foot kept him out of action. The starting quarterback role was handed to rookie Matthew Stafford, who had been a first overall league draft pick for Detroit. The end of the 2009 season was also the end of Daunte's short time with the Lions and, more important, his NFL career.

Culpepper seemed to have all the tools needed for a successful, long career as an NFL quarterback. He played the game with the precision passing and the fearless running of a future Hall of Famer. Unfortunately, injuries played a major part in his difficulties and limited his career in professional football.

From a fan's perspective, he was exciting to watch and played with a reckless desire and a big heart. He was everything one would ever want in an NFL quarterback. When he came to the Vikings as a first-round pick in the NFL Draft, he seemed to be a perfect fit for the Purple and head coach Dennis Green. His first few years with the Vikings brought out all of the high expectations, and even though the team suffered through some difficult years, Culpepper performed brilliantly in many respects.

He played in some historic games, often brought capacity crowds to their feet with his scrambling and rocket passing, and established himself early on as one of the best quarterbacks in the league. And then there came the devastating knee injury against Carolina, the eventual change in leadership and ownership of the Vikings, and the bitter parting of the ways with the star quarterback, who was never able to resurrect his career.

Still, in spite of all the turmoil and the disappointment of a promising longtime career in Minnesota, when it came time to vote for the 50 greatest Vikings, Daunte Culpepper was back at the quarterback position, settling in as one of the all-time greatest along with other Vikings signal callers Tommy Kramer and Fran Tarkenton.

His time in Minnesota was not nearly long enough. His years behind center were filled with great seasons and heartbreaking injury. But above it all, he became cemented in the hearts of the fans who have loved 50 seasons of Minnesota Vikings football.

"Daunte was built like a linebacker, but he could really throw the football. He was a good football player who was always convinced we were going to win."

—JOHN RANDLE

4,717

2004 was a very, very good year for Culpepper, who led the NFL in passes completed with 379, averaging 294.8 yards per game, for an incredible 4,717 passing yards that season.

Chris DOLEMAN

#56 | Linebacker, 1985–93, 1999

Chris Doleman admits to being a very private person. It might be difficult to convince those who had to block him of that fact. As he raced around in an opposing team's backfield, his reticence was among the farthest things from an opponent's mind.

A dominating player in the National Football League for 15 seasons, he was the fourth player selected overall in the 1985 NFL Draft. The Minnesota Vikings had the lucky pick, and there he stayed from 1985 to 1993. He was then traded to the Atlanta Falcons, where he played two years, and then spent another three seasons with the San Francisco 49ers before returning home to the Vikings in 1999 to finish out his career.

"I loved playing for the Vikings," says Doleman of the trade that sent him packing. "I was very disappointed when I was traded to Atlanta by Coach Denny Green."

Doleman grew up in York, Pennsylvania. "It was a small town with lots of down-to-earth people," Doleman continues. "My dad was a factory worker, and I come from a very humble background. My brother played for the Harlem Globetrotters, and I was pretty much a loner as a youngster. We grew up with very strong family ties and a lot of support within the family."

Chris started playing organized sports at eight years old. "My dad had a rule for us kids," he recalls. "If we signed up for something, we had to finish whatever it was." Doleman was an enthusiastic student-athlete, excelling not just at football, but also volleyball and basketball.

Chris attended William Penn High School and, after graduation, Valley Forge Military School. "I was recruited for football by just about everyone," says Chris, "and I looked very hard at Temple University before making the decision to attend the University of Pittsburgh."

While at Pitt, Doleman starred at linebacker and defensive end, where top scouts had him pegged as a promising draft pick. They were right. "I had no idea the Vikings were going to take me," Doleman says. "I have to say, as I look back on my career, it was one of the highlights to be drafted by a team with a coach as revered as Bud Grant."

He began his career in Minnesota as a linebacker, but he really came on once he was switched to the defensive end position. He had an unimpeachable reputation as an outstanding pass rusher, as well as for his ability to stay on the field. His durability kept him in 232 of a possible 237 games in his career. During eight seasons, he had more than 10 quarterback sacks per season, and in 1989 he recorded 21 sacks, fourth-most in NFL history. And he wasn't just

Chris Doleman shakes off a Patriots blocker.

Doleman puts pressure on Cardinals quarterback Tom Tupa.

"Pound for pound he was one of the strongest players in the league. He had tremendous talent and was an exceptional defensive end."

—STEVE JORDAN

sacking the quarterback; he also recorded more than 1,000 career tackles, 24 recovered fumbles, and 45 forced fumbles. His career sacks total of 150.5 ranks fourth in NFL history.

There's no doubt he played to win. In his career, he played in 17 playoff games for the Minnesota Vikings, San Francisco 49ers, and Atlanta Falcons. The teams he played on also finished first or second in their divisions during 11 of the 15 seasons he played.

Doleman was selected to the Pro Bowl team eight times. He was a First-Team All-Pro three times, a Second-Team All-Pro two times, a four-time First-Team All-NFC selection, a two-time Second-Team selection, and a member of the NFL 1990s All-Decade Team. It's little wonder that he was selected in the 2012 Hall of Fame class.

21

Doleman's 21 sacks in 1989 set the benchmark in the league that year.

Hall of Fame quarterback Warren Moon said about Doleman, following the defensive end's selection to the Vikings Ring of Honor, "Doleman is one of those rare guys, maybe one of four or five that I played against during my career—right there with Reggie White, Bruce Smith, Derrick Thomas—that you had to know where they were and set your protection accordingly.... Doleman was someone you always had to worry about, because you knew he could get to the quarterback. The amount of time and attention that went to prepare for Chris Doleman benefitted the other guys on those defensive lines. He was one of those guys that you had to make sure could be blocked in one way or another."

Remarked Hall of Famer and former teammate John Randle, "Chris Doleman had the ability to deliver the big play when you needed it. Teams had to keep an eye on him because they knew it was coming, be it at the beginning, middle, or end of the game. He was capable of making that big play. As a young guy learning the NFL from him, he did so much for me. He taught me how to be a pro on and off the field. He was quiet on the field, a leader without speaking. It was his presence that influenced games. The way he studied the game and showed his teammates the way to prepare and be a mature player made a big impact on me."

Reflecting on his legacy with the Vikings, Doleman says, "I am very humbled and honored to be selected to the Vikings Ring of Honor and to the 50 greatest Vikings team. When you are playing the game, you don't realize the impact that you may be having. So when the honor comes, it is really special."

Doleman's life off the field reflects the same type of commitment that his tremendous athletic ability gave him on the field. He wants to be a good parent and a community leader with a strong value system. "I'm still the same guy," says Chris, "and I want to be able to help and give to others to be a small part of their success."

Now that football is over for Chris, he has found other ways to contribute. He is the founder and CEO of Chris Doleman's Pro Auctions. The organization, which is informed by his experiences being a professional football player for 15 years and from his work with a variety of charities, assists charities in fund-raising, as well as raising their profiles and connecting with similar groups. "[We] help nonprofit organizations with their silent auctions and handle publicity for them," says Doleman.

Chris Doleman's athletic feats were inspiring and wonderful to watch. And his longevity in the National Football League is rare. He made huge plays on the field and was a terrific player. Given the impact he has had on the game and the impressive numbers he charted, it's fitting that on August 4, 2012, he entered the Pro Football Hall of Fame.

Doleman (center) stands with teammates at the 50 greatest Vikings halftime ceremony.

Carl Eller shows his sheer determination.

Carl ELLER

#81 | Defensive End, 1964–78

He was one of the famed Purple People Eaters and one of the greatest to ever play the game. Fans who lived in the Twin Cities during Carl's playing days had the opportunity to watch him not only achieve legendary status as a member of the Minnesota Vikings but also had the good fortune to watch him dominate the collegiate ranks as an exceptional player with the University of Minnesota Golden Gophers.

Carl Eller is one of an elite few who had the ability to literally take over a football game. His stature and athletic ability gave him the opportunity to control some of the greatest players in the NFL.

Former Minnesota Viking Jim Lindsey once said about Eller, "He was the greatest physical specimen I have ever seen. It was as if he had been chiseled out of stone."

The remark was similar to one once made by the daughter of former Vikings coach Norm Van Brocklin, Kirby Vanderyt. Kirby was a very young little girl when her father invited the team to their home one day. "I remember one party when I looked up the stairs and saw the shadow of this giant man walking in the hallway looking for the bathroom." She spoke with great passion as she described the giant visitor. "It was the great Carl Eller!"

Carl Eller was born in Winston-Salem, North Carolina, and grew up loving sports.

"I spent a lot of my early years playing sports at the local playgrounds and parks," says Eller. "I was involved in the same things as most kids—playing baseball and football. I really didn't get into organized sports until the 10th grade."

Carl's father died when Carl was only 14 years old and never got to see him play in high school or beyond. He missed something special; Eller was an outstanding high school player in addition to his collegiate and professional triumphs.

"We had some great high school teams in football," says Eller. "We won the state championship and a lot of games. I was always big as a youngster and played offensive and defensive tackle on our team. But I never gave much thought to college football at the time.

"I was a good student and worked hard," says Carl. "I was a likeable kid and president of my senior class. Some of my teachers advised me that I was a good candidate for college and that the University of Minnesota might be a good place for me to go."

Eller was recruited heavily by Murray Warmath, head football coach at the University of Minnesota. Warmath was credited with being one of the first Northern coaches to recruit African American athletes from the South—and he found a pure gem in Carl Eller.

"We called him 'Moose' for good reason. Carl was very focused on being a great player. He was very dependable, and I always felt if you needed something, he would be there to help out. He was a real gentleman."

—GENE WASHINGTON

"It was a real culture shock for me. I had barely been out of North Carolina, and it was like going to a foreign land," recalls Carl. "I was absolutely amazed by the campus and everything about the university. It was terrific and opened up all these new doors for me.

"I was never the type who planned out my football career," he continues. "It just kind of evolved for me from high school to college and to the pros. At each level, it was important to me to prove myself, not just to others but also to myself…

3
Eller played in 209 games for the Vikings, missing only three starts in his illustrious career in Purple.

"At Minnesota and in the Big Ten Conference, I was playing against the best, and it helped me greatly. When I got drafted by the Vikings, I was really pleased because there was never a doubt where I wanted to play professionally. I wanted to stay in Minnesota. I loved the area and everything about the Twin Cities."

In the early 1960s, along with fellow future Hall of Famer Bobby Bell, Eller led the Gophers toward some of the greatest seasons in the school's history. During his junior and senior seasons at Minnesota, Eller was named to the All-American teams and was runner-up to the prestigious Outland Trophy Award, given to the nation's most outstanding lineman. The University of Minnesota has since created the Carl Eller Award, which is given to the team's Defensive Player of the Year. In 2006, Carl was elected to the College Football Hall of Fame.

After finishing his eligibility at Minnesota, Eller was drafted in the first round of the 1964 NFL Draft by the Minnesota Vikings, as well as in the American Football League's Draft in the first round by the Buffalo Bills. Eller chose the Vikings and became a prominent player for Minnesota for the next 15 years. He finished his last season in the NFL with the Seattle Seahawks.

Reflecting on his career in Minnesota, Eller says, "I loved my years with the Vikings and give a lot of credit to my first coach, Norm Van Brocklin. I believe he formed the toughness of the Minnesota Vikings. He brought the attitude to the organization as being from the North and being hearty and tough. Norm wanted us to go out on the first play of the game and let the other team know who was going to be in charge. He was that way. When Bud came later on, he took some of the raw talent he inherited and molded it into a football team."

During his professional career, Eller was a Pro Bowl selection six times. He was named First-Team All-Pro five times, Second-Team All-Pro twice, and First-Team All-Conference seven times. In 1971, Eller was named the NFL Defensive Player of the Year. He was also selected to be on the 1970s All-Decade Team.

During the time that Carl Eller wore the Purple in Minnesota, the Vikings won 10 Central Division titles. He was a member of the 1969 NFL championship team and one of 10 former Vikings to have played in four Super Bowls. In his prominent Minnesota career, he only missed three out of the 212 games.

Eller was a dominant force from the defensive end position. His quarterback-sacks total is a staggering 133.5, and 130.5 came with the Vikings. In 2004, he was elected to the Pro Football Hall of Fame.

As Fran Tarkenton writes about Eller in his autobiography *Every Day Is Game Day*: "In my first tour with the Vikings, Carl was still young and did some things during games that were hard to fathom. I saw him literally throw people aside as if they were mannequins. He was magnificent in every respect…. He is a Hall of Fame player and one of the best who ever played the game. He also has a great presence and aura about him. Whatever it was, Eller had it and it was special."

Carl Eller is a true homegrown Minnesota hero. From the Gophers to the Vikings, he was a pleasure to watch. Fans will long preserve the memory of his greatness.

"[One] of my great joys has been to hear from fans that they have enjoyed my playing years. It is a real tribute when someone comes up to me and says something like that. It means a lot to me because I loved the game," says a proud Eller.

Eller is all smiles at a community charity event.

After football, Carl became a licensed chemical-dependency counselor and founded a number of substance-abuse clinics in the Twin Cities area. Now in retirement, Eller has been active in the Retired Players Association and has taken a strong position in trying to protect the future for former NFL players. He has firmly held his position that the benefits received by former players are not adequate and that the Players Association has been more involved in preserving the rights of current players rather than it has for its former players.

"It has been a great passion of mine to work on behalf of the retired players," says Eller. "There have been some things that have gone on that are not right, and I have made an effort to correct some things. I have felt it has been the right thing to do.

"Today I keep busy. I'm writing a book and look forward to my work with this, among other things," says Carl.

It's obvious how much passion he has for things in life and important causes. And it is the same passion he played with in high school, college, and in the NFL. When it came to selecting the 50 greatest Vikings, it was an easy pick. He stood taller than 6'6"—and who knows how tall with his arms outstretched when he played. He was exceptionally fast and overpoweringly strong. He manhandled opposing players. Carl is a collegiate and professional football Hall of Famer. He is a Vikings Ring of Honor selectee. He is arguably one of the greatest players to ever play professional football.

Chuck FOREMAN

#44 | Running Back, 1973–79

For many years the Minnesota Vikings were blessed with two great running backs in Bill Brown and Dave Osborn. And then came Chuck Foreman, another extra-special running back who became one of the best ever.

Chuck Foreman was born and grew up in Frederick, Maryland. As a youngster he was not involved in organized sports. He loved basketball and lived in an area from which some great basketball stars hailed. He played a lot of playground and park ball and spent a lot of time on the courts.

In the sixth grade, Foreman started to play some midget football; he excelled at it, as he did in his other athletic pursuits. He was an outstanding athlete in football, basketball, and track at Frederick High School. There, he began to perfect his pass-catching ability, becoming proficient early in his football career by catching passes out of the backfield.

He was recruited heavily out of high school and eventually decided to attend the University of Miami on a football scholarship. "I was just taken aback by the whole Miami setting," says Foreman. "I recall reading an article in *Parade* magazine and was convinced I needed to go there. They had some great athletes that had gone there that really caught my attention. I enjoyed my time at Miami and played both ways as a running back and defensive back.

"I never gave a lot of thought to a professional career while I attended high school and college. I thought I was going to be a history teacher. And I never thought I would end up playing for the Minnesota Vikings. When I first heard they drafted me and thought about the weather in Minnesota—and then later experienced it firsthand—I remember thinking, *This is craziness!*

"As cold as it was, the people in Minnesota were absolutely great. I enjoyed playing for Bud Grant and owe all of my success to my teammates. They were vital to any success that I had. I made wonderful and lasting friendships with many of my former teammates—players like Jim Marshall, Ricky Young, Ahmad Rashad, and so many others."

"We had a great relationship. Chuck was an outstanding player as both a runner and receiver coming out of the backfield."

—JERRY BURNS

Foreman powers through a pack of Cowboys defenders.

Foreman became an outstanding and versatile player for the Vikings during his eight seasons with the team. He finished his career playing his final year with the New England Patriots. During his time in Minnesota, he was named the 1973 NFL Offensive Rookie of the Year, was selected to the Pro Bowl five times, and was a four-time All-Pro selection.

He scored a record amount of touchdowns for the Vikings at the time (53) and had an incredible 73 pass receptions in 1975. One could argue that the Vikings had fielded their greatest team of all time that season, only to lose to the Dallas Cowboys in the last seconds of a playoff game on a much-disputed play.

Foreman became a terrific pass-catching running back out of the backfield. He was exceptional at making the first apparent tackler miss him, which led to excessive yardage gains and enabled the Vikings to exploit defenses.

Foreman became a catalyst for the Minnesota Vikings, moving the football up and down the field.

15

Foreman raced past the competition in 1974, leading the league in touchdowns with 15. He again topped the NFL with a mark of 14 touchdowns.

Foreman readies for the next play during game action.

He was called on many times in key situations to make the big play, and often he did.

He continues to live in the Twin Cities area and fills in from time to time as a substitute teacher in the Bloomington area. He is also involved in radio work, doing many local radio interviews and hosting an Internet radio program called *Spin It!*. Chuck is known for his insightful and unvarnished commentary on the current landscape of sports.

"It was a great honor for me to make the roster of the 50 greatest Vikings," says Foreman of the distinction. "Just to be included with so many great players is really special."

His humbleness should be no surprise to those who watched him play so unselfishly all those years.

Foreman at the Vikings 50 ceremony.

Leslie Frazier

Leslie Frazier was named interim head football coach of the Minnesota Vikings on November 22, 2010. After guiding the team to a 3–3 finish to close out the 2010 season, Frazier was named head coach on a permanent basis on January 3, 2012.

Frazier was an outstanding player in the National Football League with the Chicago Bears. Following a career shortened by a knee injury, he became a successful assistant coach and defensive coordinator in the NFL with the Philadelphia Eagles, Cincinnati Bengals, Indianapolis Colts, and Minnesota Vikings.

Upon being named the Vikings' head coach for the 2012 season, Frazier remarked, "It is a great honor and a tremendous responsibility to be the head coach of a storied franchise like the Minnesota Vikings. It is very important for us to keep progressing and continue to work hard each day to improve our football team. I am extremely thankful to hold one of 32 positions as a head coach in the National Football League.

"When the Wilf family decided to honor the 50 greatest Vikings of all time, it brought the organization together with the past and the present. During the ceremony in December of 2010, to see 50 years of greatness represented on the stage at the Convention Center in Minneapolis was an incredible moment in Vikings history."

John Gilliam reels one in.

John GILLIAM

#42 | Wide Receiver, 1972–75

John Gilliam played for the Minnesota Vikings for only four seasons, but he was a big-play receiver all the way. Teaming with Fran Tarkenton, the two were a lethal connection in the passing game.

Gilliam was born in Greenwood, South Carolina, a small town in the South. Growing up as a youngster John was always influenced by sports. "I loved to run," he says. "I used to run about eight miles every single day. I am an outdoor-type person, and running got me outside a good portion of the day.

"I went to a small all-black school and played football, basketball, baseball, and ran track," says John. "And then in high school, it was basketball, football, and track. For a variety of reasons, I only played one year of high school football. Players were not treated very well there."

Despite his brief high school football career, Gilliam received a lot of college offers, including one from Michigan State. "I was a high school All-American and lived only 30 miles from Clemson, and the coach there provided me with good information about Michigan State. I was interested, but I recognized they had Gene Washington there and didn't want to go to MSU and then not play. So I settled on South Carolina State," Gilliam said.

After starting out on the fourth team, Gilliam worked his way up, eventually becoming a starter at South Carolina State. He played split end and wide receiver. "During the third game of the season, I caught a touchdown pass," recalls John, "and never looked back. It was a great experience. I graduated in physical education with a minor in biology."

South Carolina State worked out well for John, and he became an All-American player at the collegiate level, which garnered a great deal of interest from professional teams at draft time. He was drafted by the New Orleans Saints in the second round of the 1967 National Football League Draft, 52nd overall.

Gilliam played two seasons with the Saints and was then traded to the St. Louis Cardinals, where he remained for three seasons, before being dealt to the Minnesota Vikings.

"I didn't know I had been traded [to Minnesota]," recalls Gilliam. "I got a call from head coach Bud Grant, who told me congratulations on the phone. I asked him, 'For what?' He told me I had been traded to the Minnesota Vikings. My response was, 'No, no, I'm not going to Minnesota. No way.' I told Bud I would think about it and call him back."

John finally agreed to come to Minnesota to see if he would like it. "I met Jim Marshall, Oscar Reed, Clinton

Jones, Charlie West, and many of the other guys. That was all it took, and I was sold on Minnesota," says Gillliam.

"During training camp, I met Fran Tarkenton, and we hit it off," he continues. "He threw a really nice ball, very catchable."

Indeed, Tarkenton and Gilliam made for a great passing combination. Gilliam earned Pro Bowl honors during the 1972, 1973, 1974, and 1975 seasons. After the 1974 season, Gilliam played some with the Chicago Winds of the newly formed World Football League. He returned to the Vikings for the 1975 season before spending his last two NFL seasons with the Atlanta Falcons, Chicago Bears, and New Orleans Saints.

Gilliam played in two Super Bowls with Minnesota and received several honors during his seasons in the northland. In 1972, he led the NFL in yards per catch and finished second overall in pass-receiving yardage and was named First-Team All-Pro by the Newspaper Enterprise Association. In 1973, he was named First-Team All-NFC by the *Sporting News* and the United Press International.

During the NFL off-seasons, he worked in the school system as a substitute teacher. Today, he lives in Atlanta and runs his own lawncare business. "I love what I am doing and do a great deal of my services myself. We have some nice contracts with the city and keep busy," he says.

"I keep busy with my business and spend a lot of time with my family. I love to dance, and I love to play golf. I spend a lot of my time outdoors and love to be around people.

"I remember those great years in Minnesota. The highlight of my career was being around my teammates. They were great guys, and we had great teams. And Bud, well, he was my kind of coach," recalls John.

He wasn't in Minnesota for very long, but the fans remember him fondly. They remember well the great plays, the long runs after catches, and the touchdowns. Well enough to name John Gilliam one of the 50 greatest Vikings of all time.

4,062

In only four seasons with Minnesota, Gilliam made it count, charting 4,062 all-purpose yards.

Gilliam gets ready for work.

"I learned a lot from John Gilliam. He was a classy dresser and showed me how to dress and helped me out a lot. [He was also] one of the best receivers I have ever seen."

—CHUCK FOREMAN

Bud GRANT

Head Coach,
1967–83, 1985

There is little doubt that Bud Grant had an indelible impact on his Hall of Fame quarterback, Fran Tarkenton. In fact, Tarkenton devoted an entire chapter in his autobiography *Every Day Is Game Day* to Grant and his influence. In the chapter's closing, Tarkenton writes, "Someone recently asked me if I miss Bud Grant. I don't see him very much these days or speak to him very often. I think I surprised the person who asked by saying 'no.' I don't miss Bud Grant because he is with me every day. He is part of all that I do. He was the best football coach, the best teacher, the best manager of the game, the best manager of people and the smartest person I have ever known."

In Minnesota, the surrounding region, and in the world of sports, he is known simply as "Bud." Everyone knows who is being mentioned. Everyone knows who the reference is to; it's Bud Grant, that simple. It is an honor and a reverence that his fans and former players hold for him. He is singular, just like the name by which he is referred. And he earned it.

Bud grew up during the Great Depression, and things were indeed tough for him and his family. His father was a firefighter, and his family suffered for money during the tough times. "I recall being hungry all the time," says Grant. "I used to walk on the streets instead of the sidewalks because I had a better chance of finding some loose change."

Bud was born and raised in Superior, Wisconsin. His given name is Harry Peter Grant, but he picked up his nickname, "Bud," early on in his childhood. He was an outstanding athlete and excelled early on in football, basketball, and baseball. Outside of the playgrounds and ballfields, Grant loved to hunt and fish—two things he still does quite regularly.

Grant was a star player in all three sports during high school at Superior. After graduating, he enlisted in the navy and was assigned to the Great Lakes Naval Station in Illinois. There he played on the football team coached by the now-legendary coach Paul Brown.

After his tour in the military, Grant attended the University of Minnesota, where he became a three-sport letterman in football, basketball, and baseball and earned a total of nine letters and two-time All–Big Ten honors in football.

Following his collegiate career, Grant was drafted to play professional football and professional basketball. He was the first-round, 14th overall pick by the Philadelphia Eagles in the NFL Draft and was selected 42nd overall by the Minneapolis Lakers in the 1950 NBA player draft.

Grant stayed with the Lakers for a short time and was a member on their 1950 championship team. After two seasons playing professional basketball, he agreed to cross over to football, playing for the Eagles beginning in the 1951 NFL season. During his first season with Philadelphia, Grant played defensive end and led the team in quarterback sacks. In his second season he was switched to offense, and led the team in receiving, ranking second among NFL receivers for overall yardage.

At the end of the 1952 season, his contract expired, and Grant left the NFL for the Winnipeg Blue Bombers of the Canadian Football League. At the time, he was the first professional football player to play out his option and leave for another team. While with the Blue Bombers, Grant was named a Western Conference All-Star three times. He once recorded an incredible five interceptions in 1953—in a playoff game.

In 1957, at age 29, Bud Grant became the head football coach of the Winnipeg Blue Bombers. His CFL team made six appearances in the Grey Cup championship game and won the championship four times during the 10 years that Grant coached in Canada. In 1967, he left Winnipeg to take the head coaching job for the Minnesota Vikings.

Grant has always been known for his stoic appearance and no-nonsense approach to both football and life in general. One of his most memorable moments (from a listener's perspective) came from a pregame interview he did on *NFL Today* with broadcasting personality Phyllis George. The two had been talking, when the broadcaster interrupted the interview and said, "Smile, Bud." Bud's reply, in his typical stoic fashion was, "Say something funny, Phyllis."

Watching the demeanor of Bud Grant on the sideline, it was impossible to tell by the coach's actions whether the Vikings were winning or losing. He always seemed the

Grant commands the game from the sideline.

"He was one of the great football minds of all time... and the best example of the best man I ever met."

—MICK TINGELHOFF

An avid sportsman, Grant shows off his fishing bounty.
Photo courtesy of Bud Grant

same: not too high and not too low. His consistent manner rubbed off on those around him. Players often speak of his control of a game and his tremendous management of people. He knew how to get the most out of his players and at the same time command tremendous respect.

Of course, that doesn't mean he wasn't above a good practical joke. He loved a good laugh, and oftentimes he became the victor of the prank without letting on or providing evidence that he was even a part of it.

One season, the team was out of town for the holidays. At the time, the Vikings had three quarterbacks on their roster: Fran Tarkenton, Bob Berry, and Bob Lee. Each, in their respective careers, had experienced numerous highs and lows from their former coach, Norm Van Brocklin. The team had decided to draw names among themselves in a Secret Santa–like gift-giving pool. When the players opened their presents, the three quarterbacks discovered that they each had received an identical coffee mug with the inscription on it that read, ALL IS FORGIVEN, NORM. Everyone knew Bud was behind it, but no one could prove it.

Once the entire team decided it was time to show Bud up and give him a message about his control. They contrived a master plan to send a message to the coach about his mandate that they all wear their socks at the same length. Bud wanted the white socks on the outside of the pants and to be of the same length and be pulled to only a certain height on the leg.

As they all gathered on the practice field waiting for the coach to arrive, they all had their socks on the same way and at the same length. Bud might have been pleased by their consistency—except for the fact that each player had rolled his socks down around his ankles. They all looked ridiculous—but it was a message to Bud, so he would understand.

Bud came out of the locker room and headed to the practice field. The players, dressed in purple and with their socks around their ankles, stood at attention but facing the wrong direction. They were sure this would work. They would show their coach. Grant walked out on the practice field. His socks were rolled down around his ankles just like the players'.

Fred Cox played for the Minnesota Vikings for 15 seasons and perhaps spent more time in close proximity to Grant than any other player. "I never wanted him to have to look for me," says Cox. "I wanted to always be ready." Standing next to Grant all those years taught him a lot

997

Grant was a fine player in his own right. In 1952, he caught for 997 yards with the Philadelphia Eagles, second-most among receivers in the NFL.

about Grant's knowledge of people. "He was the epitome of a person that knew how to handle others. He was a great judge of character."

Others who played for him and who have been around him tell it like it is. Former quarterback Bob Lee remarks that after meeting with Bud, "You just feel better." Paul Wiggin, former NFL great and collegiate and professional coach, who has been with the Vikings organization for many years, maybe says it best of all: "If you are fortunate enough to have an opportunity to sit down and talk with Bud Grant, when he leaves you feel like you have just completed a five-credit course."

There are a lot of stories about Bud Grant and his many decades as part of the Vikings organization. When asked about all of it, Bud replies with a masterful touch of humility. "I wasn't an airline pilot or a brain surgeon. I was a football coach in the entertainment business. It put food on the table for my family."

After all these decades and years have passed, it is Bud Grant who remains the face of the franchise. He speaks positively at all times about the franchise and supports the new stadium. He talks fondly about his greatest pride, often telling others how all of his kids and grandkids live within a shout of Winter Park, close to their dad and grandfather.

Bud has a humble outlook on all of his success. "I felt like a hypocrite in some ways," say Bud. "I am very beholden to the players who played for me. I am a reflection of what they do. It shows that they have bought into what I have been selling as a football coach. I am so appreciative of what they did on my watch. I feel like I didn't really do anything and they are the ones that made me look so good," says Grant.

His years of coaching are over but he is still around, often at Winter Park, headquarters of the Minnesota Vikings. "If I'm in town, I usually spend part of the day at my office," he says. "I keep really busy. I'm up at 5:00 AM every day and still love to hunt and fish. I can still walk through the cattail slew and get around pretty well. Being outdoors remains a big part of my life. And my family, 40 of them now, they are a big part of my life too.... The fact that they all live within a short distance of my house means a lot to me."

It is extremely telling that Grant is the only nonplayer on the list of the 50 greatest Vikings. "I give all the credit to the Wilf family for putting on the great event and process for these great players. It was really special what they did when the vast majority of the players did not play [under their ownership]," says Grant.

Jerry Burns

Jerry Burns was an assistant coach and offensive coordinator with the Minnesota Vikings from 1968 to 1985 and the head football coach from 1986 to 1991. In total, he spent 24 years with the Vikings organization. Since his retirement in 1991, Burns has been a loyal and faithful follower of the franchise.

During his time in the National Football League under Vince Lombardi in Green Bay and Bud Grant in Minnesota, Burns earned the reputation as one of the most brilliant offensive minds in the history of the NFL.

Burns coached many of the 50 greatest Vikings and had the opportunity to watch each from the sideline and/or the press box.

Burns is one of the most beloved Vikings coaches of all time. If his name enters into the conversation with someone who knows Jerry, you can almost surely count on three things to happen in the following order: First, the person will laugh a little; then, a gigantic smile will cross his face; finally, you'll hear the comment—"What a great guy!"

"Wally was a great athlete. He was an extremely smart player who could run like a deer. He...played the game with great intensity."

—ROY WINSTON

Hilgenberg takes the field with teammate Carl Eller.

Wally HILGENBERG

#58 | Linebacker, 1968–79

It didn't matter where they were or what they were doing. They always lined up and sat the same way, 60, 59, 58—Roy Winston, Lonnie Warwick, and Wally Hilgenberg. They were the linebackers for the Minnesota Vikings—playing side by side for what seemed to be forever—and they were the very best of friends, too.

The friendship between the three lasted long after their football days were over. And as coincidence would have it, when Wally was 58 years old, Lonnie Warwick was 59 years old, and Roy Winston was 60 years old—thus each man's age matched his jersey number at the same time. Longtime hunters, the trio got together often from early on. The first time that Wally joined Warwick and Winston on a day of hunting, he was told that he would need a pair of waders. After football practice, he went out and bought the waders so he would fit in with the two other linebackers. The three piled into the truck. They sat in order: Winston, on the left, driving; Warwick in the middle; and Wally on the right—60, 59, 58.

When they arrived, Wally asked the other two where their waders were. They told him they didn't have any. So after wading out to set up the decoys and wading out to pick them up, Wally figured he fit in.

Wally Hilgenberg was born in Marshalltown, Iowa. His family soon moved to Wilton, Iowa, where he grew up and went to high school. "Wally had an older brother who was an outstanding athlete, and Wally really looked up to him," says wife Mary Hilgenberg. "He spent a lot of his early youth playing baseball with his father and hunting and fishing. Wally truly loved to hunt and fish.

"Wally lived close enough to his school that he could hear the school bell in the morning. When he heard the bell, he would jump out of bed and run to school. During his school years growing up, Wally was very involved in all their sports," she continues.

Hilgenberg attended college at the University of Iowa, where he was an outstanding football player on both sides of the line, playing offensive guard and linebacker.

In 1964, Hilgenberg was drafted in the fourth round of the NFL Draft by the Detroit Lions; he was the 48th player selected overall.

"I first met Wally when he was playing for the Detroit Lions," recalls Mary. "My parents had moved to Detroit, and I went there to visit them. I met Wally at a swimming pool near where my parents were living. I asked him what he did for a living. 'I'm a Lion,' Wally told me. Later, I went to my father and asked him what a Lion was."

Hilgenberg played for Detroit for four seasons and then was traded to the Pittsburgh Steelers, who cut him. Bud Grant knew of him, and Vikings assistant coach Jerry Burns

"Wally was one of my very best friends. It really hurts a lot that he left us. We went together to Iowa and then were joined again with the Vikings in 1968. He was a great teammate and an outstanding player."

—PAUL KRAUSE

Hilgenberg takes a breather during a break for the Minnesota defense.

14

Despite playing his career on the defense, Hilgenberg still managed to put points on the board—an interception returned for a touchdown, a fumble recovered for a touchdown, and a safety.

knew Wally from his coaching days at Iowa. So the Vikings picked him up after that, and he remained with Minnesota for the next 12 seasons. It was a great match.

Wally was a steady, hard-nosed player during his career with the Vikings. He was known for his incredible aggressiveness and passion on the playing field, as well as for the bond he developed with many of his teammates. He had a reputation throughout the league as a tough guy and a powerful player on the defensive side of the ball, a player who teammates and opponents alike respected.

During the off-season, Wally worked as a manufacturing representative while in Detroit and then later in the banking industry. In 1976, he pledged to devote his life to the church. He became involved in speaking on a regular basis to many religious groups in the area and was actively involved in spreading the word and his beliefs. Their shared religion helped cement a strong bond with teammate Jeff Siemon.

In November 2006, Hilgenberg began to notice a slight twitching in his body. He was tested fully at the Mayo Clinic in Rochester, Minnesota, and was given the diagnosis of amyotrophic lateral sclerosis, often referred to as Lou Gehrig's disease.

"Wally handled it beautifully. Never once did he complain about anything. As bad as it got, he never felt sorry for himself," recalls Mary Hilgenberg. "'I have had a great life and I have no regrets,' he used to say to us. He taught each one of us how to live our lives and how to die," she says. "He would tell us it is not when you go, but rather *where* you go. This is what was important to him."

Wally Hilgenberg left his family, friends, and the football community on September 23, 2008, after a long battle. He is survived by his wife, four grown children, and several grandchildren.

In the wake of Hilgenberg's passing, there was an outpouring of love and affection from family and friends. But questions about his death remained.

"Two days after Wally died, we received a call from Boston University, wanting to study Wally's brain," says Mary. "The study is trying to determine whether brain trauma in sports may in fact cause any new type of disease that mimics ALS."

In part due to the Hilgenbergs' cooperation, researchers at the Center for the Study of Traumatic Encephalopathy at Boston University School of Medicine and the Department of Veterans Affairs have uncovered a link between sports-related brain trauma and a neurological condition that has symptoms that mimic ALS. The importance of the study and continuing research is critical in determining the connection to the disease diagnosis and the physical toll on the human body that people experience in professional sports occupations like football.

Wally Hilgenberg will be remembered much more as a person than a football player. Commenting on his selection to the 50 greatest Vikings, his widow Mary says, "I wish he could have been here to enjoy [it]. He would have been deeply honored. He loved life and played it out to the fullest."

Fans of the Vikings have been saddened by his passing, but he will always be alive in their hearts.

The Hilgenberg family gathers in 2008. *Photo courtesy of Mary Hilgenberg*

Steve HUTCHINSON

#76 | Offensive Guard, 2006–11

Steve Hutchinson joined the Minnesota Vikings in 2006 after a tour with the Seattle Seahawks from 2001 to 2005. Despite being with the Vikings for a relatively short time, he was named as one of the 50 greatest Vikings. The distinction speaks volumes for his dominance on the football field.

"I grew up in the south Florida area," says Hutchinson. "My father was a police officer with the Fort Lauderdale Police Department. I was an only child, and I had a strong upbringing from a really great family. As a youngster I loved to hunt and fish.

"I was pretty big even when I was a kid and couldn't make the football weight class, so I had to wait," he continues. "I became a tackle by the time I reached middle school.... In high school, I eventually dropped baseball, then basketball, and [played] only football by the time I was a senior."

Hutchinson was a standout player in his high school days at Coral Springs High school. In 2007, he was named to the Florida High School Athletic Association's All-Century Team, composed of the top 33 football players in the state of Florida's 100-year history of high school football. In one of the country's true hotbeds for high school football, the recognition was quite an accomplishment.

Hutchinson was heavily recruited coming out of high school—he actually got his first recruiting letter from Georgia Tech when he was just a sophomore. Growing up, he always followed Michigan football. "They were always one of my favorite teams," he says.

He attended a few football camps for high school kids, and by the time he was a junior he was offered a scholarship to the University of Michigan. He was redshirted his first

"Steve is a throwback player to a different era in pro football. There is nothing that is going to stop him. He leaves every single thing he has on the football field and is very unique for today's athlete. He will play in pain and do everything he can to avoid the trainer and training room."

—LESLIE FRAZIER

Hutchinson pushes back Lions defenders during a September 25, 2011, game.

> **"He is a Michigan guy so deserving of all the honors he has received. He is a dominant football player and a great guy!"**
>
> —JERRY BURNS

Hutchinson sets up against the Broncos.

157

Hutchinson has been an indestructible force on the football field, playing in 157 games in 11 seasons in the pros.

season in Ann Arbor and then was a starter for four full seasons with the Wolverines.

At Michigan, besides performing starting offensive guard duties, he was also the team captain for two seasons, an All–Big Ten selection four times, and an All-American twice. In addition to those honors, he was named the Big Ten Offensive Lineman of the Year and a finalist for the Outland Trophy. He also was the recipient of the Jim Parker Award from the Touchdown Club of Columbus, Ohio. Perhaps most remarkable for an offensive guard—and certainly something for which he received a thank-you from QB Brian Griese—he holds the distinction of not allowing a single sack on his quarterback during his junior and senior seasons at Michigan.

"I wasn't really sure about playing professional football," recalls Hutchinson. "As I got to my senior year, I thought that maybe I might have a chance to play." Did he ever. Hutchinson was the 17th player picked overall in the 2001 NFL Draft. "The fact that I was away from home, playing at Michigan [in college] made it a little easier to go to Seattle to play," says Hutchinson. "I was kind of used to it by then."

While in the professional ranks, Hutchinson was named to the Pro Bowl seven times, was an All-Pro selection seven times, and a two-time NFL Alumni Offensive Lineman of the Year—and he's still going. He is among the elite offensive lineman in the game; some have made the claim that he is the best active guard in professional football.

Even with all of the recognition that Steve has received, there is much more to life than just football to him. "I want to be remembered for more than just football," he says. "There are so many things in life that are important to me."

One of those things is the commitment that Steve and his wife have made to their charity work. He has been extremely active with the University of Minnesota's Children's Hospital, helping out kids who have not had the good fortune in life that many others enjoy. "We do a lot for the kids and their families around the Thanksgiving holiday," says Steve. "It really means a lot to us. I never get tired of it. I really feel deeply for these kids and the tough life they have endured."

There is a lot more to Steve Hutchinson than what is seen in the bottom of the pile on Sunday afternoons. "I'm quiet and pretty shy," he says.

Steve Hutchinson has had a great career in the NFL. He has learned how to take care of his body and works hard at his trade. "I never take it easy," he says. "I have to always be ready and to always try to improve my work."

Steve Hutchinson is a credit to the profession and committed to his craft and also to public work in helping out those less fortunate. "I want to give back and work hard to be nice to people at all times. This is important to take the extra time to sign an autograph or talk to someone. When I am done playing the game, I hope people will see me as a good person, someone who has been an ultimate teammate and friend."

With an attitude like that and his great athletic accomplishments, it's no wonder he's included among the 50 greatest Vikings.

Santa Claus (and Steve Hutchinson) are comin' to town.

Irwin dominates the San Francisco *D*.

Tim
IRWIN

#76 | Offensive Tackle, 1981–93

The honorable Tim Irwin was a solid football player who enjoyed a long career in the National Football League. He started 181 games playing for the Minnesota Vikings and split his final playing year with the Miami Dolphins and the Tampa Bay Buccaneers in 1994, recording a total of 187 NFL starts.

At the present time, Tim Irwin is on the bench. Although *this* bench is not on the sideline of a football field but in a courtroom. In 2005, he was appointed as a judge of juvenile court for Knox County in Knoxville, Tennessee. Irwin grew up in Knoxville and loved to fish and hunt whenever he had the opportunity. "It has always been a stress reliever for me," says Irwin. He was involved in youth football early on but struggled with the weight limits. He grew into his role in high school and became an exceptional football player. He was heavily recruited by many of the SEC schools, including Florida, Vanderbilt, and Kentucky. He settled on Tennessee—it a was a dream come true for him. Irwin had been a vendor at the stadium as a youngster, and "to run out on that football field as a player was one of the great moments in my life," he recalls.

As a child, selling sodas at the game as a student vendor was a passion for him, as well as a source of pocket money. On many occasions, he scrambled to earn his money during the first half of the game because by the time the third quarter arrived he could cash out his wages and plant himself into a seat to watch the balance of the game.

As a college football player, Irwin became a regular for the Tennessee Volunteers under head coach Johnny Majors. He played in the Bluebonnet Bowl in 1979, was an All-SEC selection in 1980, was twice named to the SEC's Academic Honor Roll, and was an Academic All-American his senior year at Tennessee. Because of his commitment to academics, he earned an NCAA Post-Scholarship Award.

He was drafted by the Minnesota Vikings in the third round of the 1981 NFL Draft. "I had not given much thought to professional football early on in my [college] career," says Irwin, "but then our offensive coordinator at Tennessee told me that I might have a chance to play. When the NFL Draft began, I was disappointed that I was not drafted early on, so I quit watching it and went to play racquetball. Bud Grant, coach of the Minnesota Vikings, called me, and someone had to come and find me to take the call. I was still on the racquetball court."

Irwin had plans for a career after football and set law school in his sights. He attended William Mitchell Law School in the Twin Cities and eventually transferred all of his credits to Tennessee.

Irwin enjoys a moment of rest between defensive series.

He was accepted into law school out of college, and his original plan was to go right away, but then the professional football opportunity came his way. Staying with the plan, he enrolled in the Twin Cities first and then found his way back to his home state eventually.

"I really enjoyed my time with Minnesota," says Irwin. "I had an opportunity to play for some great coaches in Bud Grant, Jerry Burns, and offensive line coach Johnny Michels. When I came into the league in 1981, I was the biggest Viking at 6'7", and I weighed 274 pounds—small in today's game. In 1994, when I left the game I was the same height and weighed 315 pounds—but my waist size was the same!

"Football is a great game, and I loved playing it," says Irwin. "But I think in doing so one can easily lose perspective on what is really important in life. I played hard every day, never tried to hurt anyone, and loved the competition. Today, as a judge in the juvenile court, I am experiencing real-life situations every single day. When I wake up every morning and go to work, I know I have a chance to make a significant difference in someone's life. This means a lot to me, and I take it very seriously."

Tim's new role has him overseeing a large staff and several juvenile court magistrates. It is the culmination of his many years of experience as a lawyer for more than two decades. Over 30,000 cases appear before him each year, everything from child support to custody disputes, juvenile delinquency cases and the termination of parental rights. "For me, my greatest thrill would be to be able to see this place close the door someday," he ruminates.

Irwin is a member of the Tennessee Sports Hall of Fame, the Greater Knoxville Sports Hall of Fame, and the National Boys and Girls Club Alumni Halls of Fame. He is also the cofounder of the Catholic Youth Football League and has sponsored the Tim Irwin/Food City Bass Tournament for more than 20 years, the proceeds of which benefit the Boys and Girls Clubs of Tennessee Valley. More than $700,000 has been raised since the tournament's inception.

Irwin proves that the measure of a football player is not just what he does on the field, but the legacy he continues to leave throughout the remainder of his life.

8

Irwin kept his quarterback safe—but he also kept his eye on the ball. He recovered eight fumbles in the span of his career, all of them to the relief of the Minnesota faithful.

"Tim always did 100 percent of what we asked him to do. He was an outstanding tackle and an extremely smart player."

—JERRY BURNS

Irwin protects Vikings quarterback Wade Wilson.

Steve
JORDAN

#83 | Tight End, 1982–94

Growing up in Phoenix, Arizona, Steve Jordan played high school football, basketball, and tennis and was outstanding in each. Jordan remembers, "I always loved sports—but life for me has always been much more than just sports. I played the piano, trumpet, and the French horn and was in the high school marching band." His father was a high school teacher during the day, a college instructor in the evening, and now teaches at the junior high level. "We used to travel all over the country as kids," recalls Steve, "attending conferences and those kinds of things with our parents."

Jordan was a good student in high school, posting close to a 4.0 grade point average. Despite being a good athlete in high school, he didn't receive much attention from colleges and universities. "I finished high school early," he says. "I was done with my senior year at the age of 16 and graduated at 17."

Steve's parents were very supportive of his football exploits but never dropped their attention from the academic part of his life. "I recall my dad saying something to me many times, like, 'You had a good game, now what about your academics?'" recalls Steve. "He knew how important school was.

"I was originally thinking I would attend college at the Air Force Academy to play tennis, but I ended up at Brown for their academics and to play football.

"Brown really challenged me academically," he continues. "It was difficult, and I had to work really hard. It really prepared me." Jordan took up civil engineering so as to develop his skills to do roll-up-your-shirtsleeves work. "I wanted to stay away [from] the all-theory type of career and enjoyed the hands-on parts," says Jordan. "I loved to get involved in technical-type projects."

"Steve was a reliable player who could really stretch the field of play. He was smart and a very tough football player and an exceptional leader on our team."

—TIM IRWIN

Jordan takes it to the Bills.

Jordan was drafted out of college in the 1982 NFL Draft as a seventh-round pick by the Minnesota Vikings. He played for Minnesota until 1994, when he retired from professional football. During his NFL career, he was selected to play in the Pro Bowl six times and was a three-time All-Pro selection.

"I had a great passion for football and really enjoyed the game," he says. "During the off-season I always stayed connected to my trade and had the opportunity to work in the civil engineering industry, which has carried me right into my career following football." He was also the player representative for the team and various aspects of the league's labor issues. All of it made him a strong team leader on the field and off.

"To be named one of the 50 greatest Vikings is quite an honor," says Steve. "Being a seventh-round pick in the NFL Draft is quite humbling. I was fortunate to be able to play the game I love at a high level and to be surrounded by so many great players," says Steve.

Although, as he says, he was "humbled by his seventh-round selection in the draft and then honored as one of the 50 greatest Vikings," the reality is, he has earned the honor in every respect. His play on the field and his team leadership on and off make the distinction well received by his teammates, fans, and coaches. He truly deserves to be one of the 50 greatest Vikings of all time.

Jordan makes the catch against the Chicago Bears.

498

Talk about productive. During his 13-year NFL career, Jordan made 498 catches, all of them with Minnesota.

Jim Kleinsasser

He wasn't selected as one of the 50 greatest Vikings. He rarely receives any publicity for his exploits on the football field, during the week or on Sunday afternoons. We don't read about his long touchdown runs or his pass-receiving yardage, and he doesn't make any of the All-Pro Teams or play in the Pro Bowl. But make no mistake about it, Jim Kleinsasser is a football player. And he wore the Purple and the helmet with the horns for 13 seasons for the Minnesota Vikings.

Kleinsasser was born in Carrington, North Dakota, where he grew up on a farm. He had a remarkable high school and collegiate athletic career, and at the conclusion of the 2011 NFL season, he retired from professional football. During his career with the Vikings, he played in the trenches as a tight end, fullback, and blocking back, where he put his tremendous blocking ability to good use.

"I was very fortunate to have been drafted by the Minnesota Vikings," says Kleinsasser. "I thought I might be going to the New York Giants, and that would have been quite a culture shock for me. I was also very blessed to have a great support system from my family throughout my football career.

"I grew up on a farm and loved doing the work, working with the cattle and in the fields," says Jim. "And I loved to play and follow sports, especially football. But I am really big into fishing and hunting also. I just love being outdoors and really enjoy the time I get with my family.

"I have played in the NFL and for the Vikings for 13 seasons, and it has been a dream come true. I was hoping to play a few years, then set a goal at eight years—but I *never* thought I would play this many."

Jim Kleinsasser left the game on his own terms, with his legs and head in good condition. Given the extreme toll an NFL career can have on the body, he left the game perhaps still in his prime. He wanted to ensure he could walk in his later years and also was concerned about the possibility of future head injuries, which many NFL players have suffered.

Kleinsasser never got much of the recognition that is showered on other professional athletes. Instead, he just came to work every day and gave it all he had. He was known by the coaches and players as a great teammate and first-class person. He also gave his time to many worthy causes in the community, becoming a team leader in this regard.

"Jim is the epitome of what a coach wants on his 53-man roster. He is a class act in every respect, a super teammate, and always has a superior attitude," says coach Leslie Frazier. "He is the type that will do anything asked of him on your football team. He is there [asking] you, 'What do you want me to do next?' Every coach wants someone like Jim on their team."

Kleinsasser's legacy with the Minnesota Vikings as a quiet leader, true professional, and friend will always be remembered. His 13 years in Purple will not be forgotten. And although Jim Kleinsasser didn't make the list of the 50 greatest Vikings, he stands shoulder to shoulder with all of them.

Kramer searches for a target in game action against the Tampa Bay Buccaneers.

Tommy KRAMER

#9 | Quarterback, 1977–89

In 1980, the Minnesota Vikings needed to defeat the Cleveland Browns to gain entry into the playoffs. It had been one of those football games where just about everything that could go wrong went wrong. The Vikings trailed 23–22 going into the final seconds of the game. Ray Scott had the call as the game wound to a close:

"Five seconds left, Kramer back to pass.... He's going deep...down the right side, to Rashad.... *Touchdown! Touchdown! Rashad, touchdown!* Kramer threw deep down the right side and Rashad caught it for a touchdown! *And the Vikings are going to the playoffs!*"

"We had 14 seconds left and had to move the ball up the field," remembers Kramer. "I went into the huddle and told the guys, 'These —— are scared of us.' We got the ball to their 46-yard line, and I told them again before the final play, 'Did I not say they are scared of us?'"

They called him "Two-Minute Tommy," and he lived up to it, bringing the Vikings from behind to victory in many a game.

Kramer was born in San Antonio, Texas, where he played his high school football at Robert E. Lee High School. He led the team to the Texas State High School Football Championship in 1971 and to the semifinals in 1972. During Kramer's two years as the quarterback of his high school team, they only lost one football game. As a senior he passed for more than 2,500 yards and threw 54 touchdown passes, while playing for the Volunteers.

"There were 11 kids in our family," says Tommy. "I had six brothers and four sisters, and I was the youngest. We lived on a ranch of 100 acres, and it seemed like all I did growing up was cut weeds and mend fences. We worked hard.

"When I registered for football in the seventh grade, there was no doubt about the position I was going to play. My dad made it clear to the team that *this boy is a quarterback*."

When Kramer was a junior, his dad told him to be ready even though he was not the team's starting quarterback. Tommy knew he had to be prepared for when the opportunity came along. "I had a net in the backyard, and I threw a lot of footballs back there," recalls Kramer. "I knew if I was going to be the best, I would have to practice hard. I would throw passes to my neighbor—some 250 a day—and in the process I put a lot of pressure on myself."

Kramer started on his high school team on defense and was the backup quarterback until the first game of the season. The starter lost several fumbles, and Kramer got his chance. His hard work and preparation paid off, as he led his team to victory. After the game, his coach sat him down

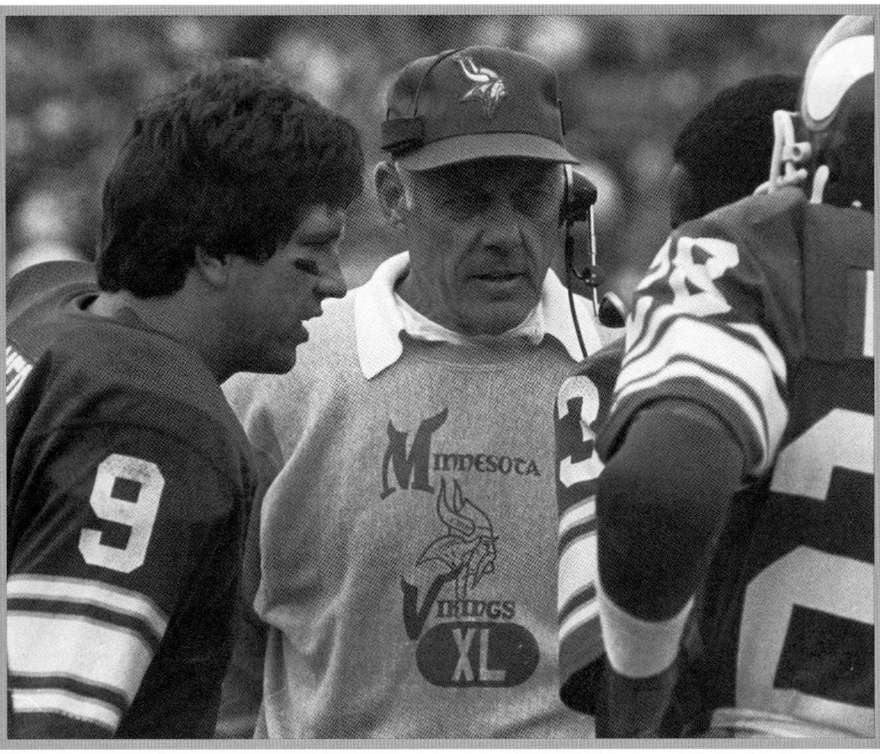

"Tommy was very involved in the game plan and was a very competitive football player. He was at his best inside the 10-yard line."

—JERRY BURNS

24,777

Kramer's 24,777 career passing yards with the Vikings are impressive—and good enough to earn him the No. 2 spot on the franchise's leading passers list.

and said, "You are my quarterback. Don't ever look over your shoulder again."

"I could have gone just about anywhere to college," recalls Kramer. "I had tons of scholarship offers. [Since] I was a kid, about six years old or so, I wanted to be just like Johnny Unitas or Joe Namath. They were my heroes. I stayed near home and went to Rice University because they were a passing team." It was a wise choice that granted him a solid ticket to the National Football League. He achieved All-American honors in 1976 following his final year at Rice.

Kramer was one of the best quarterbacks in Texas football history. He has been elected to the Texas Sports Hall of Fame. His biography there reads as follows:

"Long before the rise of the spread offense Tommy Kramer was lighting up opposing defenses as one of the greatest passers in Texas football history. The San Antonio native threw for 257 yards and three touchdowns passes while leading San Antonio Lee to a 28–27 thriller over Wichita Falls in the 1971 4A State Championship Game.

During his senior season at Rice University, Kramer led the nation in passing, was a consensus All-American and SWC selection, and finished fifth in Heisman Trophy voting. Kramer finished his remarkable career at Rice by setting school records for yards in a season (3,317 in 1976) and career passing yards with 6,197. Kramer was also named MVP of the 1977 Senior Bowl.

Tommy was drafted by the Minnesota Vikings as the 27th overall pick in the first round of the 1977 NFL Draft. "It was an adjustment from college to pro football," recalls Tommy. "The speed of the defense is what really stood out for me." Against the San Francisco 49ers, Kramer got the call to replace starter Bob Lee, who had taken over for quarterback Fran Tarkenton. It was déjà vu as Kramer lifted the Vikings from a 24–7 deficit to victory.

"I loved playing for the Vikings and Bud Grant," Kramer says. After Tarkenton retired, Kramer became the Vikings' starting quarterback for the 1979 season. He became an outstanding QB and team leader despite suffering many injuries on the football field and missing many games along the way.

Known for his late-game heroics, Two-Minute Tommy continued his aerial magic as the quarterback for the Minnesota Vikings from 1977 to 1989. Although injuries hampered his professional career, Kramer became the first player in NFL history to throw more than 450 yards on two separate occasions. He also threw for six touchdowns in one game. In 1986, he won the NFL's Comeback Player of the Year Award when he was the league's highest-rated passer and earned a trip to the Pro Bowl. Kramer's career numbers total 24,777 passing yards and 159 touchdown passes.

Kramer was an outstanding quarterback for the Vikings for 13 seasons. He brought with him a tremendous spirit and passion to every game that was enjoyed and appreciated by the fans and his teammates. When named one of the 50 greatest Vikings, he said, "It was an honor to be included on this great team of players, and I told Zygi Wilf how much I appreciated his ownership doing something like this for the players of the past and present."

One could turn that statement by Kramer around and emphasize what *he* did for the Minnesota Vikings and the fans who loved his heroics. No game was ever lost with Kramer at the controls until the final gun sounded. His nickname came about for good reason. He thrilled the crowds often with his great come-from-behind victories on his road to becoming one of the 50 greatest Vikings of all time.

Traveling for an exhibition game at England's Wembley Stadium in 1983, Kramer and teammates Scott Studwell and Matt Blair take in the sights in London.

Paul KRAUSE

#22 | Defensive Back, 1968–79

It's a superlative among superlatives: Paul Krause holds the record for pass interceptions in the National Football League, and it is a record that more than likely will never be broken. From 1964 to 1979, Paul intercepted 81 passes, an incredible feat.

Krause grew up in Burton, Michigan, where he participated in football, basketball, baseball, and track at Bendle High School. An extremely successful youth athlete, he earned a staggering 140 collegiate scholarship offers. At the time he was making his college decision, Iowa had been ranked No. 1 in football. He had some interest in attending Michigan and almost decided to go to Florida State to play baseball, but in the end, the will to be the best in football won out. He selected Iowa for its program, as well as its small-town atmosphere.

"My original goal was to attend college and play pro baseball, not football," Krause says. "But because in my junior year at Iowa I separated my shoulder playing football, it subsequently ended my hopes to play baseball on a professional level."

Instead, football called. Krause was drafted by the Washington Redskins in the second round of the NFL Draft. The 18th overall pick, he became a consensus All-Pro in his rookie season—a feat that had never been accomplished before.

During his initial season in Washington, Paul intercepted passes in seven consecutive games—and then followed that upin 1968, his first season with Minnesota, with six consecutive-game interceptions.

"I didn't get along well with one of the defensive coaches in Washington," recalls Krause. "I stayed with them for four years before being traded to Minnesota. I knew Jerry Burns, who was [then] coaching with Bud Grant in Minnesota. I used to babysit Jerry's kids, so it was a good fit for me." He

"I introduced Paul into the Hall of Fame. He is a number-one guy in my book. We go back a long way. I recruited him at Iowa. He was a great football player."

—JERRY BURNS

Krause goes off to the races after an interception.

Again showing his ability to read passers, Krause takes off wih an interception during action against the Browns.

Krause (left) poses with University of Iowa Hawkeyes co-captain Wally Hilgenberg. The two would be reunited as teammates on the Minnesota Vikings.
Photo courtesy of Mary Hilgenberg

was influenced by Grant, too. "Bud Grant was a terrific coach, and he really knew how to handle the players and the team.

"We won a lot of games in Minnesota when I was there. We had some great teams with some tremendous players over those years. Many of those guys are among my closest friends to this day."

Krause was a Pro Bowl selection eight times, an All-Pro selection eight times, and is a member of the Washington Redskins 70th Anniversary Team, the Minnesota Vikings Ring of Honor, and most prestigious of all, a member of the Pro Football Hall of Fame. He missed only two games in 16 NFL seasons.

12

Krause dominated the field in 1964, leading the league in interceptions with 12 in his rookie season.

Krause has always been vocal about how fortunate he was to be in Minnesota and play with a great Vikings defense for many seasons. His main duty assignment for the Vikings was to stop the long touchdown pass—and he was exceptional at doing it. The Vikings were great at disguising their defenses, and Krause was a crucial component. He knew how to position himself in the defensive backfield and then move quickly once the play was under way. He understood all of the game nuances and rarely seemed to be out of position. He made big plays at key times.

During the off-season, Krause was involved in many successful business ventures. He has been involved in real estate, an ice cream store, golf courses, and motorcycles, among other things. In addition, he has kept busy as a Dakota County (Minnesota) commissioner for the past 17 years.

A big part of Paul's life has also been taking care of his wife, who was severely injured in an automobile accident about 15 years ago. His devotion and special caring for her has occupied an extraordinary amount of time through the years.

Paul was not just a great player for Minnesota but one of the best defensive backs to ever play professional football. He had some of his very best years wearing Purple, and Minnesota will always be grateful to have had him.

Larsen lets loose against the Detroit Lions.

"Gary Larsen is a man's man. He actually looked like a Viking back when we played.... He was an excellent football player, a real success story."

—STU VOIGT

Gary LARSEN

#77 | Defensive Tackle, 1965–74

He will always be remembered as a dominant run stopper on one of the most famous defensive lines in the history of the National Football League.

A Fargo, North Dakota, native, Larsen attended a one-room schoolhouse, "a little country school called Clearview Grade School," he remembers. "Grades one to four were in the same room, and grades five to eight took another room.

"I grew up on a wheat and sugar beet farm," he continues. "I spent a lot of my time feeding the chickens and hogs. I drove a tractor and did all the things that farm kids do growing up."

In high school he played eight-man football, basketball, baseball, and threw the shot put. "In my playing days, I was considered big as a football player but small by comparison to today's player. I grew pretty fast. In the eighth grade I was 5'8" and weighed 160 pounds, and by the time I was a senior in high school, I was 6'5" and weighed 260 pounds."

After high school, Larsen went into the marine corps for three years and then came back to college, where he played football at Concordia College in Illinois. "I never gave a thought to professional football," he recalls. "My plan was to be a teacher. I wanted to get an education and become a physical education teacher. Then one day, a scout from the Los Angeles Rams came to Concordia and looked at some of our game film…and became very interested in my potential as a football player in the National Football League."

By the time the draft came along, other teams had also taken notice of the bruising tackle. "I thought I was going to be drafted by the Baltimore Colts because they had expressed interest, but the next morning I got a call from the Rams," he says. "They had drafted me in the 10th round as the 133rd pick in the 1964 NFL Draft."

The following year, the Vikings drafted a wide receiver named Jack Snow. Snow wasn't happy landing in the snowy tundra of Minnesota; he wanted to play for the Rams. Subsequently, a trade was worked out, and Larsen was one of the players sent over to the Vikings from L.A.

"With the Vikings, I always had the feeling that we worked our way up to the top," Larsen says. "We all knew where we had come from—as part of an early expansion team—and we never wanted to go back to the tough times we had gone through.

"Many of us were together for a long time and had played under head coach Norm Van Brocklin. Norm was a great football mind but an extremely emotional coach. He was very different from Bud Grant, which we all got to experience when Bud arrived in 1967."

Larsen was a formidable force on the Vikings defensive line and teamed up with Alan Page, Carl Eller, and Jim Marshall to become one of the most notorious and feared defensive linemen in all of professional football. They were known everywhere as the Purple People Eaters. The moniker, a reference to the 1958 song performed by Sheb Wooley, was certainly apt—Larsen and company simply devoured everyone in their path.

The devastating foursome had a motto by which they lived and played: "Meet at the quarterback." No matter who the opposing team, the quarterback always had a target on his back.

The amount of superlatives the group earned is staggering. As a group, they were virtually unstoppable. All four of them were multiple Pro Bowl selections—and in 1969, *all four* got the nod, a rare feat among defensive linemen. That year, true to their motto, they sacked opposing quarterbacks an unthinkable 50 times. They played together in three Super Bowls in four years. And the Minnesota defense gave up the fewest points to opponents in three consecutive years (1969–71), topping several other defensive categories along the way.

133

Proof positive that draft position is no predictor of success in the NFL, 133rd pick Larsen became a two-time Pro Bowler with the Vikings.

The Purple People Eaters were a crucial part of the successful teams the Vikings fielded in the mid-1970s. Even though the team never was able to capture the grand prize of a Super Bowl championship, their defense is still regarded as one of the best in NFL history, alongside the Fearsome Foursome of the Los Angeles Rams of the 1960s and early 1970s, Pittsburgh's Steel Curtain in the 1970s, and the New York Jets' Sack Exchange of the 1980s.

Larsen was a dominant player at shutting down the opponents' running game. He was big, strong, and played with a tremendous amount of heart. He played with the Vikings until retirement in 1974.

"I knew it was coming," recalls Larsen. "Many of us older players were leaving. Players like Milt Sunde, Grady Alderman, and Bill Brown were being replaced. We had been together and played for a lot of years."

Larsen spent his off-seasons in the Los Angeles area (his wife is a native Californian) and made it his permanent home after his playing career. He did go back to school and got that teaching certificate he'd originally planned on, too. Ultimately, he became a commercial auto salesman.

Now in retirement, his life is quieter. "My wife and I play golf together a lot. We have four daughters and nine grandchildren, and that keeps us pretty busy. I have been fortunate. I still see my old teammates some and treasure my years with them—I see Jim Marshall from time to time and occasionally Milt Sunde, Grady Alderman, and Bill Brown. Their friendships have been special.

"[Being] selected as one of the 50 greatest Vikings…is the biggest honor I have ever had," he continues. One could make the argument that the honor was the fans', who got to see Larsen's spectacular feats on the gridiron for 10 years.

"He was one of the Purple People Eaters, a strong defensive player who kept us in field position with his great defensive play."

—JERRY BURNS

Carl
LEE

#39 | Defensive Back, 1983–93

Born in Charleston, West Virginia, Carl Lee was raised in the small town of Vandalia. "It seemed like there were only around 100 people in the whole community," remembers Lee. "I think I knew just about everyone. We all lived in about a two-block area."

Lee's family later moved to the Spring Hill section of Charleston. "I spent a lot of my time growing up playing on the street. It was my world. My very earliest of memories are out there on Greenway Avenue playing sports," Lee continues. "I was playing [football] constantly on the street, in the backyard, throwing and catching."

It seems Lee caught the football bug from an early age. "I was obsessed with football. It's all I thought about. [As] far back as I can remember, I have wanted to play professional football. I was a big fan of the Cleveland Browns and really followed them during the Leroy Kelly era. When the Browns lost, I can remember crying with disappointment.

"My dad was involved with football also and played semipro ball with the Charleston Rockets, which was really a huge deal back then. I just simply lived for football.

"My dad helped me out. He would throw the ball to me as often as he could, and I would run out for passes, throw it back, dive and catch the ball. It was all I wanted to do. Once I started to play organized football, I wasn't really big. But my dad told me that the bigger they are, the harder they fall, so I took him at his word. I would go looking for the big guy on the field to make his point," says Lee.

"I never got overly confident in my abilities and never paid much attention to how good a player I was. But I recall standing on the 50-yard line at the Pro Bowl and thinking, *To be here I must be a pretty good player*," recalls Lee.

Lee describes himself as an average player in junior high school. He tried to make the varsity in the 10th grade but didn't make the cut; he was deeply disappointed. In the 11th grade, the high school defensive backfield coach told Carl he would put him at the safety position until he found someone better. He never did. Carl received an honorable mention for his play that year, disappointed he didn't make First-Team All-Conference. He pledged to make that list the next year. For motivation, he actually posted the All-Conference Team names on his wall. By the time he finished his senior year, he made the All-Conference Team and earned several other awards.

Carl had the opportunity to go to Virginia Tech and could have walked on at many other colleges. In the end, he chose Marshall University. Sonny Randle, head coach of the Marshall program, told Lee early on, "If you can play, I will guarantee you a shot at the pros." It was all the motivation Lee needed.

Lee reels in an interception against the Miami Dolphins.

"Carl Lee was very fast and had extremely good cover skills. He worked hard at the game and was a self-made type of player."

—SCOTT STUDWELL

"Again, all that was on my mind," said Carl, "was I wanted to play pro football. And I was willing to pay the price to have the opportunity. I had no interest in being a doctor, dentist, teacher, or anything else. I wanted to play professional football."

Carl shined at Marshall and was confident going into Draft Day in 1983. He anticipated being drafted in the third or fourth round but wound up very discouraged when he was passed over. He waited and waited, asking friends and family to leave him alone until he (hopefully) got that call. Finally, the phone rang. It was the Minnesota Vikings, calling to tell him they had taken him in the seventh round (he was chosen 186th overall).

"I remember thinking, *Did this just happen? Did I get drafted by the Minnesota Vikings? It is finally going to happen. I am going to play pro football*," Lee remembers fondly. "All these other things—like high school, college, the draft—they were all in my way. Now I was going to get to play out my dream.

"It *was* a dream. When I first came out of that tunnel and stood by Bud Grant, it was unbelievable. I was where others had been, like Jim Marshall, Chuck Foreman, Fran Tarkenton, Carl Eller, Gene Washington, and so many others.

199
Lee's 799 career tackles are representative of his attraction to ball carriers and receivers.

A bruiser in the making.
Photo courtesy of Carl Lee

"It's hard for me to talk about it today because people will quickly realize how much I miss the game. I worked hard at it. I was always in peak condition. I worked out five days a week and really put everything into the game."

Lee left little doubt in the minds of fans that he played his heart and soul out. During his 11-year career with the Vikings, Lee was named to three Pro Bowls. In 1988, he made eight interceptions—finishing just behind Atlanta's Scott Case for league-leading honors. That same season, Lee returned not one but two of those interceptions for touchdowns, an NFL-best mark. He finished his career with 31 interceptions and a total of 799 tackles.

After his retirement in 1994, Carl became the head football coach at West Virginia State, where he remained for 10 years. He does a daily radio show on ESPN in Charleston and remains involved with the university through community outreach, doing liaison work for the county parks and recreation departments.

"I love what I am doing and still work out regularly to keep in shape. I have to get my run in every day," says Carl. "It's still what I do.

"I am still in awe of being named as one of the 50 greatest Vikings," reflects Lee. "I am now affiliated with the names I looked up to as a kid. Marshall, Eller, Tarkenton. They are on the team with me."

Bob Lurtsema

When the totals and tabulations came in, and the list of the 50 greatest Vikings of all time was announced, there was one popular name that didn't make the list. In a way, it was fitting. The man known as "Benchwarmer Bob" made his reputation, after all, by riding the bench. Now one of the greatest stories in Vikings lore has another dimension—another starting lineup from which Lurtsema is excluded.

Despite Lurtsema's I-can't-get-no-respect legacy, he has become one of the most fiercely loyal and devoted Vikings alumni in the team's 50-year history. He has been around the organization for more than 40 years, going from the field (and, okay, the bench) to one of the Vikings' strongest ambassadors.

But the irony of his beloved status is that he is known for his *lack* of football prowess—presumably that which landed him on the bench. As it happens, nothing could be further from the truth. The fact is, Bob Lurtsema was an outstanding football player. One has to be to survive in the National Football League for 11 seasons.

Lurtsema spent five years with the New York Giants, five years with the Minnesota Vikings, and part of two seasons with the Seattle Seahawks. What many often forget is that he backed up the Purple People Eaters themselves—perhaps the greatest defensive linemen in the history of the game.

Hall of Fame quarterback Fran Tarkenton, who played with Lurtsema in New York and later with the Vikings, described Lurtsema as the "best defensive lineman" on his Giants teams.

With Minnesota, Lurtsema wore his "Benchwarmer Bob" tag with dignity and good humor, often proudly speaking of his career on the bottom of the depth chart. And the hilarious Twin City Federal commercials promoting and glamorizing his benchwarmer status were instrumental in securing his lock on fan popularity. Who can forget the commercial, "Bob Lurtsema Day at Metropolitan Stadium"? The camera pans the stadium and reveals not a soul in the stands. Instead, a dog chasing Bob off the field keeps attendance from being zero.

In *A Tradition of Purple*, I wrote an account of Lurtsema being sent into a game early, an unusual occurrence:

> On the first play, he crashed through the line in ferocious style, sacking Lions quarterback Bill Munson on the turf. Delivering a fierce hit, Lurtsema had done his job to perfection. It was a terrific play—one for the highlight films and a lifelong memory. Lurtsema knew what a great play he had made. His mind raced with thoughts of highlight reels.... It was exactly what he was paid to do, and he did it during primetime in an unforgettable fashion. The drama and excitement, however, were not long-lasting.
>
> As Lurtsema lay on the ground enjoying the moment, the Detroit quarterback looked up at him and said, "My...are we that far behind already that you're in the game?"

It just wouldn't be right to have a book written about the first 50 years of Minnesota Vikings football and not somewhere mention Bob Lurtsema. He was a terrific player, a good sport, and will forever be a devoted fan of the Purple. No matter what the vote, Bob Lurtsema will always be one of the greatest Vikings.

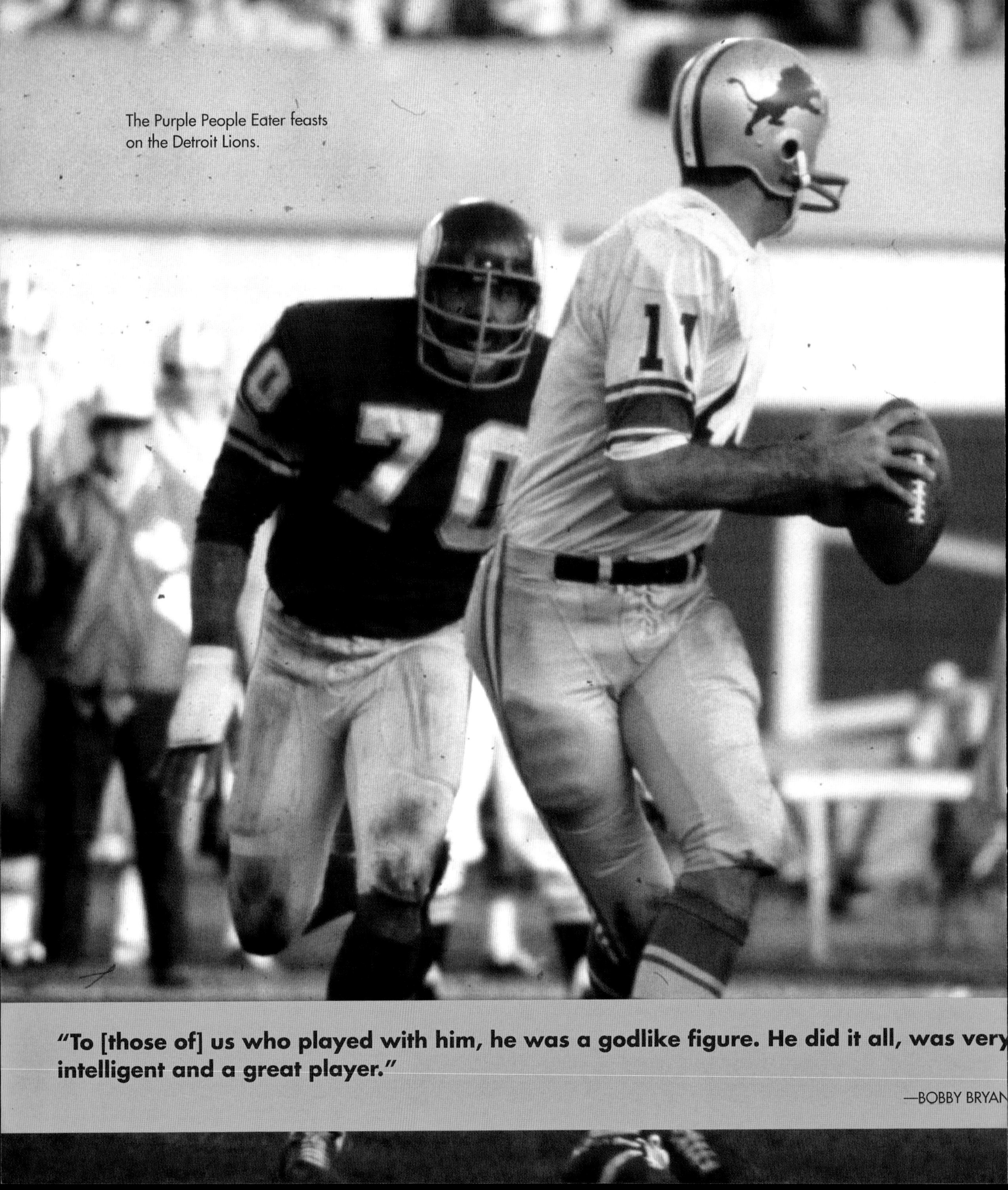

The Purple People Eater feasts on the Detroit Lions.

"To [those of] us who played with him, he was a godlike figure. He did it all, was very intelligent and a great player."

—BOBBY BRYAN

Jim MARSHALL

#70 | Defensive End, 1961–79

Where does one start to talk about Jim Marshall? Perhaps it's best to begin at the beginning.

Jim was born in Danville, Kentucky, and spent some of his early years in Wilsonville, Kentucky, before eventually moving to Cleveland, Ohio. As a youngster, Jim loved sports. "I liked to run as a kid," says Marshall. "I was outside all the time, playing anything and everything I could in the neighborhood. I loved to play tag and really prided myself on the ability to be the last one caught in the game. The first [organized] sport I got involved in growing up was track, but I got into football and other sports too."

As a student-athlete, he excelled at everything. Jim earned 16 letters in high school at East High School in Columbus. Suffice it to say, he was heavily recruited by colleges and universities after being named All-City, All-State, and All-American.

Legendary Ohio State football coach Woody Hayes wanted Marshall at OSU in no uncertain terms. "He just simply said to me one day, 'Jim, you can go and look at any school you want to look at, but just remember one thing: you *are* going to Ohio State,'" Marshall remembers, laughing.

Marshall was a standout player on the Buckeyes team, with which he won one national championship and a Rose Bowl. He earned All-American honors and is a member of the esteemed Ohio State O Hall of Fame.

He passed up his senior year in college to go pro and went to Canada to play for the Saskatchewan Roughriders of the CFL. He had been drafted by the Cleveland Browns of the National Football League, and after one year of playing in Canada, he joined the Browns.

At Cleveland, Jim played under the tutelage of another legendary coach, Paul Brown. But with NFL expansion on the horizon, every team was losing personnel to make way for the new teams. Jim was left off the protected player roster in Cleveland and was picked up by the Minnesota Vikings in the league's expansion draft.

Before joining the Vikings, Marshall was called into duty with the National Guard. He had been in training at Fort Leonard Wood, Kansas, when he developed encephalitis. He was in an induced coma for several weeks and suffered significant weight loss. Recovered, but well out of his prime physical condition, he reported to the Vikings at 212 pounds.

He soon made up the weight loss; it was as if he hadn't lost a single step. He started 270 straight games for the Vikings, never missing a single start during his career in Purple. This feat did require him—on two separate

Marshall and Eller leave the field.

occasions—to check himself out of the hospital and go from his hospital bed to the game (once when he had pneumonia and the other, ulcers).

"I got my work ethic from my father and my grandfather," says Marshall. "They taught me how to work every day. When you have a job, you do the job. You never let anyone down because you are not there. Injuries—it didn't matter to me. It was more important to me to play through the pain and perform than to sit out and suffer from not participating. It was the way I was taught and brought up.

"I was fortunate to play with some great teammates and a great coach in Bud Grant. We have a wonderful bond between us, and I treasure it. Bud and I have had great respect for each other." Marshall recalls one time when he and teammates succeeded in putting one over on Grant, a very rare feat.

"Bud found out that I had a gun with me at training camp. He told me to put it away except for one special time [when] he would call on me to use it. When the team was leaving camp to drive to the [Twin] Cities for a football game, Bud would have all the players line their cars up in front of the dorm. He would then call on me to start them off by firing my gun like a starter pistol. We knew Bud would then call the state patrol and tell them the team was coming and to stop the speeders...

"We found out that Bud was using studded tires on his vehicle all year round. The Minnesota law required the studded tires to be removed after the snow season. So we called the highway patrol and told them to stop Grant [for his] illegal tires. We sure enjoyed passing Bud as he was stopped...on the side of the road."

Jim played for the Vikings from 1961 to 1979—a remarkable 19-year career. A two-time Pro Bowler, he was a member of the famed Purple People Eaters along with Gary Larsen, Alan Page, and Carl Eller. Together, they composed one of the greatest defensive front fours in the history of professional football.

In Fran Tarkenton's *Every Day Is Game Day*, he describes Marshall in no uncertain terms:

No one wore the purple colors more proudly than Jim Marshall.... Jim was a great athlete and as smart a player as I have ever played with or against. We used to play chess and

19

Of all of his feats, this one might be the toughest for players to match. Marshall gave 19 years of service to the Vikings, landing him just one year shy of the NFL's record.

I could never beat him—he always won. And he always brought his A game with him on Sundays. I believe I can challenge anyone intellectually, but I tried many times to top Jim, and I never could. Whether it was a game of chess or an argument about virtually anything, Jim was the best. I could never get that step ahead of him.

Jim...arrived at the Vikings weighing just 215 pounds—and he was going to line up against the likes of Jim Parker from Baltimore, who weighed 280! The Browns had cut him in camp, and he had come to us a week later. Can you imagine that? The Browns didn't think he could play. I would not have liked to have been the person who pulled the trigger on that decision.

Jim never had a bad game. We were at opposite ends of the locker room, and his passion and desire just exuded across the room. I admired him so much. He played in 282 consecutive games, 270 of them with the Vikings! Just think of that, 282 games over 20 years in the National Football League, and he isn't in the Hall of Fame? It's criminal! It was a great privilege, honor, and wonderful experience to have had the opportunity to watch Jim Marshall play the game. And to call him my teammate and friend will always be very special to me.

Marshall attends the 50 greatest Vikings ceremony.

He indeed belongs in the Hall of fame. It cannot be said more clearly. He has earned it. Hall of Famer Jim Langer, former great Miami Dolphins player who spent the last seasons of his career with Marshall in Minnesota late in his career, feels strongly that Marshall should be beside him in Canton. In Langer's endorsement of Marshall for the Hall of Fame, he describes Marshall as "one of the greatest players in NFL history, a playmaker on the defensive team [who] can ruin your offensive game plan" and "an NFL player's player." Marshall may well get his gold jacket someday.

Outside of football, Marshall has enjoyed an interesting life. Whether it be mountain climbing, skydiving, or burning money to stay alive while trapped in a blizzard in the mountains, Jim has survived it all. "I have [jumped] out of airplanes 2,067 times," he says. Apparently, Marshall approaches his leisure activities with the same commitment and fortitude he took with him to the ballfield.

Jim has also found many ways to give back to the community, giving of himself for numerous charitable causes. He has worked with the Courage Center, the Special Olympics, and has established many programs that aid and assist young people. For his outstanding charity work, he received the Minneapolis Urban League's Outstanding Lifetime Achievement Award.

Fans of Marshall and the Vikings can now enjoy his new venture: the opening of a new sports bar/restaurant in Two Harbors, Minnesota, called Viking Legends. For a man who stands uncategorically as a Vikings legend in his own right, the name is apt.

"It is a tremendous honor to be put in that category," says Jim. Commenting on his selection to the 50 greatest Vikings, Marshall is succinct: "What more could one ask for?"

Randall
McDANIEL

#64 | Offensive Guard, 1988–99

He may have been the best offensive guard ever to play the game of professional football. He was recognized for his high school play, his collegiate play, is a member of the College Football Hall of Fame, the Minnesota Vikings Ring of Honor, the 50 greatest Vikings, and the Pro Football Hall of Fame. But if you were to ask Randall McDaniel what he would like to be best remembered for, it would resoundingly be that he made a difference in the lives of children.

Those who know him well think of Randall as a gentle giant. He is a devoted family man who seeks out the opportunity to assist those who are less fortunate and in need of help and guidance.

He grew up in Avondale, Arizona, about 15 miles west of Phoenix. "My parents never pushed sports on us," he remembers, "but I did spend a lot of time in the streets participating, mostly with older kids.

"Most of my friends got involved with Pop Warner football, but I was too big," says Randall. "I had to pass on it until high school, when I started as a sophomore playing tight end and defensive linebacker. Early on in my youth, I [had] played most sports except football. Later I was into just about everything, playing football, basketball, and baseball. I also ran track at Agua Fria High School."

When the collegiate recruiting season began for Randall, it was his standout play on the basketball court, not the football field, that garnered the most attention. "I grew up in Arizona, so I knew I was going to go to Arizona State. It was an easy decision for me," he says.

Once at ASU, McDaniel turned his attention to football. He was a solid player, anchoring the offensive line and playing in three bowl games for the Sun Devils. In 1986, Arizona State finished the season with a 10–1–1 record, which included a victory over Michigan in the Rose Bowl. It is McDaniel's fondest memory from his college days. He started 39 consecutive games with the Sun Devils and won the Morris Trophy as the Pac-10's Top Offensive Lineman in 1986. McDaniel was also a two-time All-American and is a member of the ASU All-Century Team.

As the NFL Draft approached, Randall figured he would be taken by the Oakland Raiders, who had shown a lot of interest in him. He was selected 19th overall by the Minnesota Vikings, and his career in Purple began.

"I was honored to be selected by the Vikings," he remembers. "The first time I went to meet the organization, I was taken around by offensive line coach John Michels. I asked him where head coach Jerry Burns was, and he pointed him out to me. I recall saying to him, 'No really, where is Coach

McDaniel runs interference for teammate Herschel Walker.

McDaniels (64) and the Purple go to work.

Burns?' John looked me and said, 'That's him.' I thought he was pointing to Burgess Meredith.

"Seriously, though, I loved playing for Jerry Burns. [He was] a tremendous coach and person. And as for John Michels, I owe all my success to him as my line coach. I was very fortunate to have Jerry, John, and later Denny Green as my coaches."

For someone who thought he might not be drafted, McDaniel had an illustrious career in the NFL. In total, he played in 222 games and was elected to play in the Pro Bowl 12 times. He was a nine-time First-Team All-Pro selection and a 10-time First-Team All-NFC selection. In addition, McDaniel was named to the NFL's 1990s All-Decade Team.

Yet with all of these awards and honors under his belt, when he was named to the 50 greatest Vikings list, he responded with the ultimate humility: "It is a great honor to

222

Talk about an iron man. In 14 seasons in the NFL, McDaniel played in each of 222 of 224 possible games, paving his way to Canton.

"Randall was a great player with high expectations for himself and the team. It was as important to him, if not even more, to become a great teacher working with kids."

—ANTHONY CARTER

be selected, but I still think there are a lot of players better than me."

McDaniel's real passion in life has been his career off the football field. Working with kids in the classroom has been a highly motivational calling for one of the greatest players to ever play the game of football.

"I want to make a difference to kids," he says with profound sincerity. And this is not just lip service; McDaniel has been working for several years in the elementary schools in the Twin Cities.

"It started by just reading to kids in the classroom, and [I] worked [my] way into substitute teacher roles and working every day with kids who need the help and motivation to succeed.

"I work with kids in basic skills classes and in special education. It gives me tremendous energy to know I am doing these kids some good. I try to give the kids a message that they have to make a difference in others' lives. I will give it my best and try to help any child that I can.

"I truly enjoy every aspect of what I am doing in the schools. I am just as big a kid myself that you would ever find anywhere. I always have a great time working with the youngsters. They are really important to me."

McDaniel's second act is an inspiration to all those who know him. His tenacity, humbleness, and commitment are virtues that served him well not just in the game of football, but beyond. His work in the schools brings another side of this great athlete forward—the side he would like to be remembered for. His success in the classroom likely will match or become even greater than his success on the field. It certainly is his goal.

McDaniel reads a story to some of his students.
Photo courtesy of Randall McDaniel

Keith Millard gives chase to 49ers quarterback Joe Montana.

Keith MILLARD

#75 | Defensive Tackle, 1985–91

For opposing quarterbacks approaching the line of scrimmage and looking things over, seeing Keith Millard ready to go into attack mode was among the most unwelcome sights. Millard played the game with a penchant for violence and mayhem. He knew how to rush the passer and destroy what was in his way. And he did it for a long time as a professional football player in the National Football League.

Millard was born and grew up in Pleasanton, California, south of San Francisco. "I was a soccer player first," says Millard. "I was a tall, skinny kid growing up and didn't give a lot of thought to football, let alone ever playing it professionally.

"I came from a family of 11 kids, and we had a lot of family time together. We did camping and a lot of backyard activities growing up. To this day my family is very important to me. We have six kids and try to be involved with them as much as possible."

Keith played high school football at Foothill High School and collegiately at Washington State. As a freshman at WSU, he played tight end before moving to defensive tackle. He became a starter in his junior year. As a senior, his play with the Cougars was excellent; he was selected First-Team All–Pac-10, and he won the Morris Trophy as the Pac-10's top defensive lineman.

Millard was drafted by the Minnesota Vikings in the first round of the National Football League's 1984 draft. He elected instead to play for the Jacksonville Bulls of the United States Football League.

By the next season, he joined the Vikings, where he became an instant success story on the defensive line. Millard played seven outstanding seasons with Minnesota, from 1985 to 1991.

"I really liked playing for the Vikings, and I loved playing for Jerry Burns," says Millard. "We had a lot of good players, and it was absolutely awesome to be there. I hated playing in the USFL, so this was just perfect for me to be in Minnesota and in the National Football League."

While with the Vikings, Millard was selected to play in the Pro Bowl twice and recorded 58 career sacks and two interceptions in 93 games in the NFL. He was named First-Team All-Pro twice, Second-Team All-Pro twice, and selected to the NFL's 1980s All-Decade Team. Millard was additionally the 1989 NFL Defensive Player of the Year, and the UPI NFC Player of the Year, having set an NFL record during the 1989 season when he recorded an incredible 18 sacks as a defensive tackle, a feat never before accomplished. And, after only one year in the USFL, he was named to the Second-Team All-Time USFL Team.

Quarterback Randall Cunningham tries to get rid of the ball before Millard arrives.

Early in the 1990 season, Keith suffered a damaging knee injury that caused him to miss the remainder of the season. Being the type of player that he was, he fought hard to make it back on the playing field, but he was never able to regain his dominance. He finished his NFL career with the Seattle Seahawks and Green Bay Packers in 1992 and the Philadelphia Eagles in 1993.

Once he retired as a player, his passion and love for the game brought him into the coaching ranks, where he has also excelled as a defensive line coach. His coaching career has taken him to the Los Angeles Dragons of the SFL in 2000, the San Francisco Demons of the XFL in 2001, the Denver Broncos from 2001 to 2004, the Oakland Raiders from 2005 to 2008, followed by the Tampa Bay Buccaneers.

"I love the coaching profession and really liked working with the Buccaneers. We had a lot of good young players, and it was really great to work with them."

Millard has demonstrated his passion for the game at all levels, and he now translates that passion to new players rising through the ranks. But it is as a man, not just a football player, that he wishes to be remembered.

"I want to be thought of by others as a good person," he says. I hope to be seen as a great family man and a caring individual. I want to take every opportunity that I have in life to be able to assist others in any way that I can. It frustrates me when I see people who do not take their abilities seriously or do not give life or their profession their best. I am a goal-setter, absolutely driven to be successful. I want that for others also."

On the football field there was never a doubt about Keith Millard's passion and love for the game. During the time in his career before the devastating injury, he was one of the very best.

53

Seemingly a one-man sack machine, Millard recorded a robust 53 sacks while with Minnesota.

"Keith had unbelievable passion for the game of football. He had tremendous quickness and...was a dominant force on the defensive line."

—SCOTT STUDWELL

Randy MOSS

#84 | Wide Receiver, 1998–2004, 2010

If you want to judge a player's ability in the National Football League by numbers and accomplishments, Randy Moss' records speak for themselves. By no less authority than the NFL itself, in 2009 Moss was rated No. 65 among the NFL's best players of all time. In his first season, he was named the Associated Press NFL Offensive Rookie of the Year and Pro Football Writers Association Rookie of the Year. He was the NFL Alumni Receiver of the Year in 1998, too. Among the many awards and distinctions he received are the 1997 Fred Biletnikoff Award and the Paul Warfield Trophy. He was a five-time All-Pro selection, 2003 NFC Player of the Year, and the PFWA Comeback Player of the Year in 2007. Moss made the New England Patriots' All-2000s Team, as well as the NFL's All-Decade Team for the 2000s. And he was named to six Pro Bowls.

The list goes on. After an illustrious NFL career, Moss holds many records for his offensive production. He made more than 950 receptions for almost 15,000 yards and 153 touchdowns. There is no doubt—he certainly left his mark in all of professional football.

Moss was born in Rand, West Virginia, and played his high school ball at DuPont High in Belle, West Virginia. He was an outstanding athlete, lettering in football, basketball, and baseball. He also ran track, in which he was West Virginia state champion in the 100- and 200-meter dashes. As a football player, he led his team to the state high school championship twice—in 1992 and again in 1993.

But Moss' star status didn't come from just playing at the wide receiver position for which he is known in the professional ranks. He also played defensive back, returned all kicks, and was the punter and place-kicker for his team. In 2009 he was named by *Parade* magazine as one of the 50 greatest high school football players of all time.

Moss originally planned to attend Notre Dame on a football scholarship, but he ended up at Marshall University following a short stint at Florida State University. At

"He was the greatest wide receiver I have seen play the game. He could really catch the football."

—JERRY BURNS

Moss beats not one but two Lions defenders.

Marshall, he set many of the school's records, including most games with a touchdown catch in a season with 14 and most consecutive games with a touchdown catch at 13. During the 1997 season, Randy made a remarkable 25 touchdown catches for Marshall. By the end of his collegiate career, he had caught a touchdown pass in every single game in which he participated.

Moss was selected by the Minnesota Vikings as the 21st overall pick in the 1998 NFL Draft. As a rookie in 1998, he was one of the main reasons the Minnesota Vikings scored a then-record 556 points. He was a deep receiver threat like very few who had come before him. He was extremely fast and had tremendous jumping and leaping ability. He was as feared as any wide receiver before or since.

Opponents' game plans against the Vikings shifted drastically; they became centered around the team's ability to keep Moss out of the end zone. It was not a good time for defensive backs in the NFL if the Vikings were on their schedule. Moss had the ability to turn

5

Demonstrating why he is Hall of Fame bound, Moss has put up five seasons in which he led the league in receiving touchdowns.

Moss signs autographs for the Minnesota faithful.

Randy Moss poses with VIPs at a charity event aiding the homeless.

the game around in an instant, to literally take over a football game with his tremendous pass-catching abilities.

In March 2005, the Minnesota Vikings traded their prized receiver to the Oakland Raiders. After two years in Oakland, Moss was traded again, this time to the New England Patriots, where he had a phenomenal season in 2007, catching 98 passes for 1,493 yards and an NFL-record 23 touchdowns. After a slightly down year in 2008, he followed with another incredible year in 2009, catching 83 passes for 1,264 yards and 13 touchdowns.

During the 2010 season, Moss was dealt back to the Vikings, but he was released before the end of the year. He finished the year with the Tennessee Titans in 2010. He retired following the season but has signed a contract to play in 2012 with the San Francisco 49ers.

Randy Moss has always been known for his outsized achievements on the football field. But he was also outstanding, if barely noticed, for his excellent work in the community. He has been involved in and financed many charity functions through the years, everything from fundraising to hosting autograph sessions to benefit charitable causes.

He has expressed a sincere desire to see smiles on the faces of children. In 2005, he started the Randy Moss Celebrity Charity Bass Tournament, and in 2008, he formed the Links for Learning Foundation to aid the neediest students in West Virginia. Over the years he has done so much behind the scenes; he simply has never really gotten the recognition he deserves. It may sound strange, but he never really wanted the attention.

There is no disputing Moss' inclusion on the 50 greatest Vikings roster. Volumes could be filled with his achievements on the football field. Put simply, he is one of the greatest wide receivers who ever played the game. Some might say he was the best ever, as dangerous a receiver running down the field as any other. He made more exciting plays than multiple Hall of Famers made in their entire careers combined. He could run, jump, leap, and make seemingly impossible catches look easy.

Minnesota was fortunate to have this incredible receiver play in the Twin Cities during his prime years. He put on quite a performance that earned him notoriety as one of the 50 greatest Vikings.

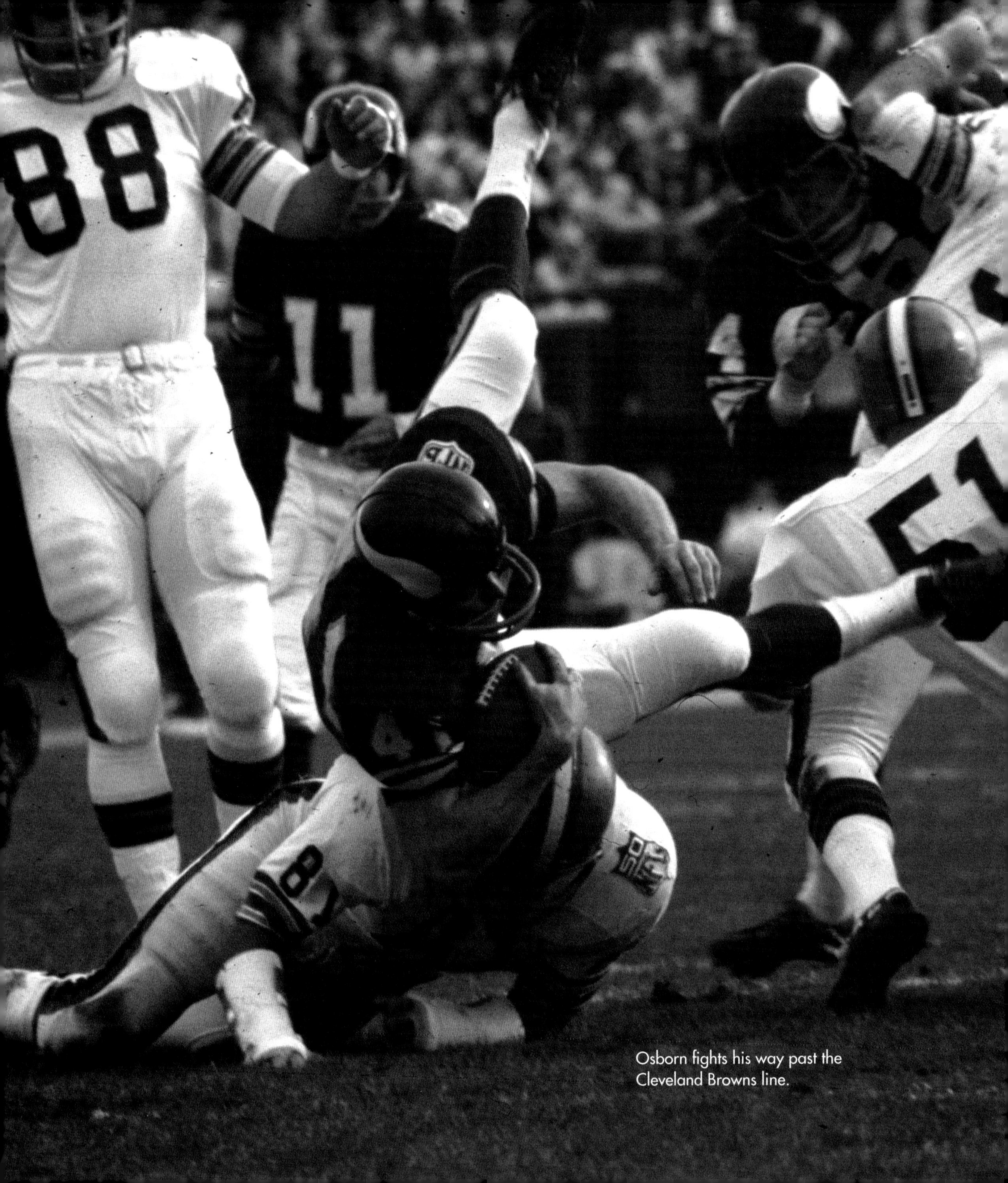

Osborn fights his way past the
Cleveland Browns line.

Dave OSBORN

#41 | Running Back, 1965–75

No one can sum up the feeling on those Minnesota Vikings teams better than Osborn himself, who says, "We would have played for free. We truly loved the game that much."

Reflecting on his younger days, Osborn says, "I don't know, maybe it was my enjoyment as a kid playing 'pump, pump, pull away' that got my juices flowing to become a running back someday. The game involved a lot of running up and down the field trying to make it from one end to the other without being tagged by another player. I used to dodge, run, weave, and usually I was tough to catch. I was always pretty fast. Even as a kid, I could outrun most of my friends. In fact, I'm told my grandfather was a fast runner; my dad was fast. My kids are fast, and my grandkids are fast, too. It's just in our genes. It's not something that can be taught. You either are or you're not."

Dave Osborn grew up on a farm in Cando, North Dakota, a small town with a population of about 1,800 back in the late 1950s and early 1960s. He lived the reality of a *Little House on the Prairie*–style schoolhouse. "It was a one-room school," says Osborn, with "grades one through eight in the same room. In fact, there were some grades where we didn't have anyone, and then there might be only two or three students in others."

Dave and his family—two sisters, one older, one younger—grew up about 12 miles southwest of town and about two miles from school. "It was really different from today," he continues. "I often rode a horse to school and easily adapted to the small-town charm of the little school. Then again, I didn't know of anything else. I can recall sitting in class and maybe two students would be called up to the teacher's desk to learn about third-grade math that day, while the rest of us would be studying our fifth-grade English. It's the way it was for us."

During the summer, Dave played Little League baseball—and it happened that the coach was also one of the high school coaches. By the time Dave entered high school in the ninth grade, his Little League coach who had also been the high school football coach, was then heading up coaching duties for basketball. Right away, he saw something special in Osborn: he saw a gifted athlete who could really run—and run with a tremendous abundance of energy. He had a motor inside him that never stopped.

"I knew very little about football," says Osborn. "We didn't have television at our house, so I had no aspirations of someday playing even college football, let alone professionally." With encouragement from his Little League coach, Osborn went out for high school football at Cando while in

"Dave was a tremendous running back from the University of North Dakota. He never gave up on a play. There is not a bad bone in Dave Osborn's body. He is simply a great human being."

—FRAN TARKENTON

the ninth grade, but he failed the physical because of a heart murmur. Instead, he spent the season as the team's student manager.

The next season, he passed the fall physical but was told by his doctor to take it easy. Dave likes to claim he took the doctor's advice, and with a big grin says, "So I took it easy for the rest of my life."

His junior year was shortened by a collarbone injury, and after playing in a few games during his senior year, Cando was hit with a major snowstorm. "We had a big storm, and they cancelled the rest of the season. But I had a few good games," he remembers. A few good games is putting it mildly; Osborn's powerful running netted him a scholarship offer at the University of North Dakota and an appointment to the Air Force Academy. He took the North Dakota offer.

After an illustrious college career, Osborn was drafted in the 13th round of the 1965 NFL Draft. The conventional wisdom is that if a player is drafted that late, the majority of the teams—often including the teams that drafted you—don't think you can play. Osborn proved them all wrong.

"When I went to training camp with the Vikings in 1965, all I had to do was take a look at stiffs like Mick Tingelhoff out there, and I knew I would make the team," says a smiling Osborn, well within hearing range of his friend Mick. Osborn did make the team and was a valued running back for 11 years. He'll be the first to tell you that he loved every minute of it.

"I played with a great group of players," he says, "and most of them remain my friends to this day. We played for each other as a team."

Osborn hoped to make it 12 years with the Vikings but failed to survive one of the final cuts at the end of training camp. Thinking his career was over, he found out during a hunting trip that a rival team had interest. It took a phone call from Green Bay Packers coach Bart Starr to get Dave back in uniform, this time wearing the hated green and gold.

His love for the Purple and sense of humor kept his friendships intact when Green Bay visited the Twin Cities. In a particularly nefarious move, knowing the Vikings, under Bud Grant, would arrive at the old Metropolitan Stadium much later than the visiting Packers, Osborn immediately entered the vacant Vikings locker room. He found the lockers of some of his old friends and tied their jerseys, socks, and anything else he could find in knots.

During those days at the stadium, both teams were stationed on the same side of the field. Osborn heard jeers

1,244

Gaining 972 yards on the ground and another 272 yards receiving, 1967 was a banner year for Osborn, and a career-best.

Osborn poses—with a fresh kill—in front of the one-room schoolhouse he attended in Cando, North Dakota.
Photo courtesy of Dave Osborn

throughout the game from his former teammates. "We know it was you, Osborn, and we will get you for it," they chanted. After the game, several of his former teammates chased him across the field, captured him, and stuffed him into an adjacent snowbank.

It was a different time in pro football that stands in stark contrast to the game today. "We didn't get paid much," Osborn remembers, "so we all had to work during the off-season. I went to work for the *St. Paul Pioneer Press* selling retail advertising. From there I got into the car business and at one time owned a car dealership. Eventually I went to work for Copy Duplicating, selling office machines. I finished up my other career working for Jackson Landscaping.

"The most I ever made for one season was $60,000," he continues. "Not much compared to what players make today. In fact, I kept track of all my earnings during my 12 NFL seasons, including playoffs and Super Bowls, and my total earnings were not quite what the minimum now paid to rookies [is] for one season."

But as Osborn tells it, it was never for the money; it was all for the love of the game. He was an exceptional running back in the National Football League for a staggering 12 seasons—a truly long career, particularly for a running back. He rushed for 4,320 yards for the Vikings and became one of their most durable players. Teaming up in the backfield with Bill Brown, the two combined toughness with exceptional running, blocking, and pass-catching abilities, making them one of the best backfields in the NFL.

Osborn's years with the team, combined with his commitment to every aspect of the game, make him stand among original men in Purple. He epitomizes what the Minnesota Vikings were all about in the early years. He represents a passion for the game second to none. He is all about honor, toughness, loyalty, and the desire essential to being a football player.

Alan PAGE

#88 | Defensive Tackle, 1967–78

Alan Page traveled from Canton, Ohio, to Notre Dame, to the National Football League, only to end up back in Canton, Ohio, enshrined in the Pro Football Hall of Fame. He is one of just three natives of Canton to share the honor, along with Marion Motley of the Cleveland Browns and Dan Dierdorf of the St. Louis Cardinals.

Today, as a justice on the Minnesota Supreme Court, he has exemplified the virtues that have made him a success on the field and off.

"I was a shy kid growing up," recalls Page. "I was kind of a loner, and not a very good athlete. I can recall being the kid no one wanted on their team when sides were being chosen, always the last kid picked. But I really enjoyed school. My parents stressed education and learning. However, my true learning came later when I was in law school.

"When I was younger, I…was involved in a lot of different things. I liked to read, enjoyed music, and played the tuba in the junior high school band. I also played the piano and really learned discipline understanding music. It was in the ninth grade that I began to participate in football. I had tried some basketball a year before, and that was a disaster. The theater was also something that interested me in high school."

As a high school athlete, Page got plenty of attention for his football heroics. He was recruited by about a dozen schools for football, but he chose to play at Notre Dame because of their sterling reputation not just on the gridiron, but in the classroom. "I felt I had the best chance for a strong academic program at Notre Dame," says Page. "They had what I was looking for in college. I knew by then that I wanted to study the law and become a lawyer. I think I got my first interest in the law profession from watching *Perry Mason* on television. I felt it was important work. I also remember reading a case in the newspaper that intrigued me. It was the *Brown v. the Board of Education* case that got a lot of attention in 1954."

Page's sights were set squarely on the law as his collegiate career began. "At the time when I was finishing high school and decided on Notre Dame, I never had given professional football a thought. It wasn't until I was almost finished with my eligibility that I started thinking about it as an initial career. I did really enjoy playing the game but initially didn't give any thought to going into coaching or continuing playing after college," recalls Page.

While at Notre Dame, Page was an All-American and a leader on the national championship Fighting Irish team in 1966. In 1967, he played in the East-West Shrine Game.

Page puts pressure on Lions QB Greg Landry.

"Alan is a great individual, family man, and wonderful friend.... He was such a tremendous player. It was an honor to play with him."

—JOHN GILLIAM

Twenty-five years later, he received game honors and a Hall of Fame induction for the East-West Game. Indeed, his legendary status as a college player is so great that a bronze statue of Page is at the Hall of Fame Gate at Notre Dame Stadium.

After his senior season, the NFL came calling. Page was drafted by the Minnesota Vikings in the first round of the 1967 NFL Draft. The addition of Page was a shot in the arm for the still-fledgling team.

He played with Minnesota for 11½ seasons, until 1978, and then finished his last three and a half years in the NFL with the Chicago Bears. During his 15 years playing professional football in the NFL, Page was a dominant player. He was a four-time NFL/NFC champion with Minnesota and was selected to play in the Pro Bowl nine times. A six-time First-Team All-Pro selection and three-time Second-Team All-Pro selection, he was also a First-Team All-Conference selection an incredible 11 times.

215

Page's 215 NFL starts rank first all-time among defensive linemen.

Page was named to the 1970s NFL All-Decade Team and was the 1970 Defensive Player of the Year. In 1971, he was named the National Football League's Most Valuable Player, at the time unheard of for a defenseman.

He was also named the 1971 Associated Press Defensive Player of the Year, the 1971 United Press International NFC Player of the Year, the 1971 NFC Defensive Player of the Year, and was selected to the Minnesota Vikings 25th and 40th Anniversary Teams. Alan has been elected to the Vikings Ring of Honor, and his No. 88 is retired by the team. In short, his pro football career was nothing short of phenomenal.

During Alan's years in the NFL, he tried a few things in the off-season before settling in on a law degree and work in the legal profession. One of those jobs was selling cars for J. Kline Chevrolet. He learned early on that it was not his calling. During his tenure, he managed to sell only one car while working as a car salesman. He bought the car for himself.

His work with the NFL Players Association brought about a sincere interest in labor law and helped to solidify his career after football. He graduated from the University of Minnesota Law School in 1978, did some private-practice work, and also worked for the attorney general's office in Minnesota.

In 1992, he was elected to a vacant seat on the Minnesota Supreme Court. He has since been reelected in 1998, 2004, and again in 2010. His current term is his last, as there is a mandatory retirement age of 70 on the court. As a judge on the Minnesota Supreme Court, he has exemplified the virtues that have made him a success on the field and off.

The honors that Page has achieved beyond the football field are numerous and noteworthy. His work in the community with the Page Foundation has been extraordinary. Many of the awards he has received over the years have been direct recognition for his incredible community work.

Despite his successes as a professional football player, Page would suggest that his true passion lies far off the field. It is what he likes to talk about—his hope for the future, that children get the support systems that so many of them desperately need. This need lies at the heart of his foundation.

Through the Alan Page Education Foundation, with the help of contributions and fund-raisers, underprivileged children of color have been provided the resources to make their educational dreams become a reality. The program supports the Page Scholars who are aided and assisted, but in the process, these same scholars then provide the assistance to others like themselves.

From the purple and gold to the robes of a state supreme court justice, Page has worn his uniforms with dignity, grace, and above all, the selflessness of a man who recognizes a greater calling beyond himself.

Page wears a new uniform.
Photo courtesy of Alan Page

AP is on his way to a phenomenal NFL rushing career.

"Adrian is a great player. He does things on the football field that have never been done before. He loves to have fun and is also a tremendous family person."

—ANTOINE WINFIELD

Adrian PETERSON

#28 | Running Back, 2007–Present

When the commissioner of the National Football League stepped up to the podium to announce the seventh selection in the 2007 NFL Draft and said, "With the seventh pick in the 2007 NFL Draft, the Minnesota Vikings select Adrian Peterson, running back from the University of Oklahoma," it seemed as though the roar from the Vikings faithful gathered in the practice facility at Winter Park might blow the roof right off the place. Going into the draft, Peterson was unquestionably the choice of the fans.

And what a choice it has been, as Adrian Peterson has proven in just a short period. He has established himself as one of the elite running backs in the league. Some NFL experts felt Peterson had been selected too high in the draft, given a shoulder injury that might prove problematic. As it turns out, they were dead wrong. And the six teams that passed on Peterson before the Vikings got him now have to justify their oversights.

Adrian Peterson has proven beyond a shadow of a doubt that he is the real deal. By the time he's done, he may well be the best running back in NFL history. His punishing running style and burning desire for greatness has cemented him as a favorite of his teammates, coaches, and fans. Every time he touches the football, one can hear the fans take a collective breath, watching to see how far he will travel and if he will take it all the way to the end zone.

Peterson is a running back on a single mission: finding the end zone. "I just love to run and love the competition involved in football," says Peterson. "When I used to run track, I felt the same way about that."

Peterson runs with a tremendous passion for the game on the football field, but off the field he is perhaps even more committed to doing the right thing and inspiring youngsters. "I am very blessed to be in the position I am in as a professional football player, but my real mission in life is to help others," says a passionate Peterson. "I really enjoy talking to kids and trying to be a good role model for them.

"I tell kids to never lose faith in their abilities and to keep God in their prayers and be a good person…. I want people to look at me and think I am an honest, decent person with a lot of integrity. I want to be myself and be nice to others and come across as a genuine person. That is really important to me. I want the kids to look up to me and say that 'he has a big heart and helps people in their lives.'"

Peterson is so humble, it seems at times he might not even realize he is the superstar that he is. "I might do a lot of things on the football field, but in reality, I am just a home

Peterson scores against the Panthers.

body," he says. "I'm a really low-key person. I like to watch a lot of television, play DVDs, and I really enjoy movies."

Peterson was born in Palestine, Texas. Both of his parents were exceptional athletes in high school and college, though his father's athletic career was derailed by an accidental gun accident, which caused him a significant leg injury.

From the time Adrian first stepped onto a football field, he was a star. He played Pop Warner football and took his great athleticism to the high school fields. He set track-and-field records at Palestine High School, while also playing basketball and football. As a junior and senior at Palestine, his dominance on the football field became apparent.

During his junior year, he carried the ball 246 times for a school-record 2,051 yards for an average of 8.3 yards per carry and 22 touchdowns. He then obliterated his junior-season marks, rushing for 2,960 yards and 32 touchdowns in his senior season, averaging an astounding 11.7 yards per carry. He was so revered in Palestine, opponents would ask him for his autograph after games.

Some believed Peterson was good enough in high school that he could have made the transition straight into professional football, had the rules allowed it. To say that many schools were interested in his services in the collegiate ranks would be a gross understatement. Peterson chose to play college football at the University of Oklahoma because

296

Peterson's breathtaking performance on November 7, 2007, against the San Diego Chargers is the best single-day rushing performance in NFL history.

he wanted to be on a team that he felt had a legitimate shot at a national championship.

He started breaking records almost immediately, rushing for 1,925 yards during his freshman season. He finished second in the Heisman Trophy balloting that year and was the first Oklahoma freshman football player to ever achieve All-American honors.

His sophomore and junior years at Oklahoma were fraught with some injuries. He had a high ankle sprain, which limited his performance his second year in college, and then suffered a broken collarbone during his junior year. It was this injury that brought some skepticism to his draft status for the NFL.

As a Minnesota Viking he has already set some phenomenal team records, including a franchise-best 224 yards on 20 carries against the Chicago Bears. Later in the 2007 season, he broke that record by achieving an NFL-best 296 yards rushing in a game against the San Diego Chargers.

Peterson has become a major threat to opposing teams, and their collective game plans hinge on finding ways to stop the explosive runner. In 2011, NFL.com ranked Peterson No. 3 among all active players in the National Football League.

In just a handful of years in the league, he has been awarded many honors, including 2007 Associated Press NFL Offensive Rookie of the Year, 2007 Diet Pepsi NFL Rookie of the Year, 2007 Second-Team All-Pro, 2007 Pro Bowl Most Valuable Player, 2007 Pro Bowl selection, 2008 Best Breakthrough Athlete ESPY, the 2008 NFL Rushing title, 2008 First-Team All-Pro, 2008 FedEx Ground Player of the Year, 2009 First-Team All-Pro, and 2010 Second-Team All-Pro. He has also been selected to the Pro Bowl in four consecutive seasons. Many records bear his name in the National Football League, with undoubtedly more to follow.

He is as driven a player as has ever stepped on a football field. He is a threat every single time he touches the football. But he truly is so much more.

It appears that he has never had an unkind word spoken about him. He is beloved by the fans, respected to the fullest extent by his coaches and teammates, and takes a hard look at himself as he constantly tries to be a good person and help others along the way.

"Sometimes, the demands for my time for autographs and so forth can get pretty overwhelming," says Peterson, "but I try to use as much patience as I possibly can. I truly want to treat people the same as I would like to be treated. I realize the effect that I can have on someone if I am not nice or patient with them. I want to set a good example."

Peterson has been just that, a dual threat—great on the football field and off. Asked what he wants to do when his playing days are over, Peterson says, "I think I want to get into real estate. I think it would be interesting to be involved in this type of work focused on land and properties."

Near the end of the 2011 season, he suffered a serious knee injury that ended his season one game early. With his physical and mental makeup, it is anticipated that he will make a full recovery and continue to dominate defenses around the league.

Peterson tosses the ball around with a special fan.

John RANDLE

#93 | Defensive Tackle, 1990–2000

It must have been intimidating for opposing quarterbacks to approach the line of scrimmage and look over the line at John Randle, with his face painted and fire in his eyes. And that was nothing compared to what he looked like once the ball was snapped.

An undrafted player, it's remarkable to think that he was passed over by every team in the league in the 1990 NFL Draft. In an era where size matters, many of them thought he was just too small. He wasn't fast enough or quick enough or good enough, the experts said. It was with that "conventional wisdom" that the draft boards were filled, and Randle, the defensive tackle from Mumford, Texas, remained at home.

Flash forward 20 years. John Randle is elected to the Pro Football Hall of Fame in Canton, Ohio, and is widely regarded as one of the greatest players of all time. What happened? How could every team in the National Football League miss on him? The answer is simple. There was no method or meter to measure the size of John Randle's heart. There was no method to measure his desire and his competitiveness.

John was raised in the cradle of high school football—the state of Texas—in a very rural community called Mumford. His family struggled for money. "We lived in a very small three-room house," recalls Randle.

"I loved sports and played football, basketball, and baseball," Randle continues. "My heroes growing up were Tony Dorsett and Roger Staubach of the Dallas Cowboys.

"It was tough growing up and trying to get to school for practice. We lived about 11 miles away, and I would have to ride two separate buses every day and then, after practice, try to hitch a ride home. Most of the time I would get home late at night."

John played high school football in Hearne, Texas, and went to Trinity Valley Community College in Athens, Texas. He eventually transferred to Texas A&I University in Kingsville. He was an outstanding player, but he never really caught the eye of the professional scouts.

His older brother made it to the NFL before him as a linebacker for the Tampa Bay Buccaneers. John tried out with the Bucs after the player draft but was not signed to a contract. Instead, he ended up signing with the Minnesota Vikings during training camp.

"I always had the belief that I could make it in professional football," says Randle. "I just wanted the chance to prove it. Frank Gilliam from the Vikings gave me a shot with the team, and I am forever thankful to him for believing in me. The Vikings' defensive line coach was Paul

Randle crushes the competition.

"There was something really special about John. He was just an outstanding player in every aspect of the game. His desire on the field was remarkable."

—JOEY BROWNER

15.5

Randle's take-no-prisoners attitude was never more noticeable than in 1997, when he led the NFL in sacks with 15.5.

Wiggin, and I got a tremendous amount of encouragement from him and others.

"I was undersized for a football player, especially for a defensive lineman.... No one gave me a chance to make it before the Vikings signed me. I wanted to show all those in doubt who passed me over. It was a tremendous incentive for me to succeed."

By 1993, John was selected to play in the Pro Bowl. He had come on as one of the most dominant tackles in the National Football League, recording double-digit sacks in nine seasons. He was a force on the field with a motor inside him that never quit running. He also had a reputation for being a constant heckler of opponents, as well as for his intimidating visage. He would wear elaborate face paint during games to further psych out his opponents. Some of them have commented that Randle was simply unblockable.

"I always gave it my very best and worked hard at taking care of myself physically to always stay healthy," says Randle. That constant effort paid off. Randle played for Minnesota from 1990 to 2000 and finished his career in Seattle from 2001 to 2003. While in the NFL he was selected to play in the Pro Bowl seven times and was a six-time First-Team All-Pro selection. He was selected to the NFL's 1990s All-Decade Team, is a member of the 100 NFL Sacks Club, a member of the Vikings Ring of Honor, and in the Pro Football Hall of Fame.

"I am tremendously humbled by the honors I have received," says Randle. "I think about the beginning, when I first came here, and then to be named one of the 50 best players is really something. I am deeply honored by it all. It will be something my kids and grandkids will be able to enjoy as well.

"As far as the Hall of Fame goes, what an unbelievable honor. This is a team that, once you are on it, you cannot be cut, waived, or traded. You are a member of this team forever."

With his playing days behind him, Randle has found a different motivation. "Today, I spend a great deal of my time with my family trying my best to be a good husband and father to my children. I love to play golf and work hard at the game every day. I try to do as much as I can in the community and spend some of my time working in schools with disabled kids. I have a really good day when I can give of my time to do something like that to help out young kids.

"Now that football is over for me, I am really looking forward to the rest of my life with my family and friends. I don't want to look back, just forward in life. Everything has been a true honor and privilege for me," says John.

The true privilege has been for the fans, coaches, and teammates who have had the opportunity to watch John Randle play the game of football. He turned the motor on at Vikings training camp in 1990 and never turned it off. His unique presence on the field was incomparable. It was all part of the enthusiasm and love he brought to the game during every day of his football career.

Randle (front row, right) and Chuck Foreman (back row, fourth from left), volunteer with members of the community.

The Coaches: **A Timeline**

Norm Van Brocklin (1961–66):
The first head coach in franchise history. His overall record was 29 wins, 51 losses, and four ties.

Bud Grant (1967–83, 1985):
He led the Vikings to four Super Bowls and became the face of the franchise. His overall record was 168 wins, 108 losses, and five ties.

Les Steckel (1984):
The former assistant coach was head coach for only one season. His overall record was 3 wins and 13 losses.

Jerry Burns (1986–91):
One of the great offensive minds in NFL history. His overall record was 55 wins and 46 losses.

Dennis Green (1992–2001): Green had a significant number of winning seasons. His overall record was 101 wins and 70 losses.

Mike Tice (2001–05): A former player and assistant coach, he was head coach for five years. His overall record was 33 wins and 34 losses.

Brad Childress (2006–10): Improved his win total in every season except his last. His overall record was 40 wins and 37 losses.

Leslie Frazier (2010–Present): The former assistant is in his second full season as head coach. His overall record is 6 wins (and counting) and 16 losses.

"Ahmad was an unbelievable receiver. He is a great person and was an extremely smart player for us."

—JERRY BURNS

Rashad breaks into his route during game action.

Ahmad RASHAD

#28 | Wide Receiver, 1976–82

It was the play that shocked them all. Trailing with only a few seconds left in the game, Tommy Kramer launched a bomb down the sideline to Ahmad Rashad, who made a spectacular catch of the ball and backed into the end zone for the winning touchdown. The unbelievable play was good for a victory—and it advanced the Vikings into the playoffs.

It will always rank near the top as one of the greatest Hail Mary passes in league history, a true football miracle. But tell that to the two Vikings involved in the play.

Kramer, the Vikings quarterback, believed it would happen. He was confident in the huddle that they were going to win. Rashad feels similarly.

"For us, it was just one of many great plays," recalls Rashad. "It was a last-minute game-winner, but if you think back to our history at the time, it happened a lot that we would pull games out at or near the end. It was what we did back then. We had a great football team, and I expected myself to make those kinds of plays. It was what we were accustomed to doing.

"I used to feel that if I didn't have a good game, we were not going to win, so I made it a point to give all I had every game we played.

"It was quite a game, no doubt about that. And fans in both Minnesota and Cleveland still, after more than 30 years, remember how the game ended. I can recall several times on airplanes people coming up to me and saying, 'I'm from Cleveland and I hate you,'" says Rashad, laughing.

Ahmad Rashad was born in Portland, Oregon, as Bobby Moore. (In 1972, he converted to Islam and changed his name to Ahmad Rashad.) He grew up in Tacoma, Washington. "I never saw a pro football game until I played in one," recalls Rashad. "I mostly hung out around the Boys Clubs and was involved in all kinds of activities as a youngster. I really liked school and really liked life.

"I enjoyed just about everything in life growing up and still do today. I was always wondering what was out there in the world, because I wanted to experience it. I was just excited about life and living every day. I was fortunate that sports gave me the opportunity to do so many wonderful things."

Reflecting on some of his early influences, he says, "I have met some great people in my life. People like Mrs. Barnard, my seventh-grade English teacher.... I kept in touch with her for many years. She was a great teacher and a magnificent person. I learned a lot from her.

"I am thankful to so many people in my life. Fran Tarkenton is one of them. If it were not for Fran, my career would have ended in Minnesota before it even started. The

Vikings were going to let me go shortly after they obtained me from Seattle because they thought I was injured. Fran would not let it happen.

"I met Fran as a rookie in the off-season in Palm Springs. He was my hero. Everyone wanted to be Fran Tarkenton. We talked some and both thought at the time that it would be great if we could play together someday. He was so famous and such a great player.

"I remember shortly after I joined the Vikings, a friend asked me if I knew Fran Tarkenton. I told him that I did and that we were teammates. His response was, 'Yes, but does Fran Tarkenton know *you*?'"

The respect and mutual affection between the two great players is obvious.

"In 1976, I had the opportunity to play with one of the most gifted pass receivers I have ever seen on a football field," recalls Tarkenton in his autobiography, *Every Day Is Game Day*. "His incredible athleticism, balance, and gracefulness were breathtaking to watch. He was truly poetry in motion. As fate would have it, he was also moments away from never playing a down for the Minnesota Vikings. His name was Ahmad Rashad."

Tarkenton continues, "We were desperate for a receiver when Rashad showed up for practice one day. He stepped on the field, and before long I was like a kid in a candy store. He was coming up with everything I threw at him. He ran outs, posts, hitches, quick outs, and he beat everybody on our team! I had never seen anyone like him before. I came home that night and told my wife I had just met the best receiver I have ever thrown the ball to in my life.

"I arrived at practice the next day busting at the seams. I was eager to get out there and throw to him. When I got there, Rashad was sitting in the locker room with his street clothes on. That worried me. I asked him what he was doing, and he told me the coaches asked him not to get dressed and to wait there until they returned.

"It was not a good sign," writes Tarkenton. "I found out it was head coach Bud Grant that had asked Rashad to stay dressed and that general manager Mike Lynn was concerned about Rashad's knee." Tarkenton responded, "I don't care if he can't push off! Did you see what he did on the field? He beat every player we had out there! He caught everything I threw at him! No one could cover him! He was better with a bad leg than anyone we had! What else does he have to do?"

1,156

A reliable receiver for more than a decade, Rashad posted the best season of his career in 1979, with Minnesota. He caught 80 passes for 1,156 yards.

Tarkenton asked Bud to get Mike Lynn on the phone, and the two talked briefly. Fran made his point to Mike. "I said, 'Mike, if Ahmad Rashad is not dressing for practice today, then I'm not dressing for practice,'" recalled Tarkenton. And the rest is history.

"I love Ahmad Rashad as a player," says Tarkenton, "but mostly because he is an exceptional person."

"I loved playing for the Vikings and Bud Grant," recalls Rashad. "Bud really understood me as a player and even more so as a person. He is the greatest manager of men of any person I have ever met. I recall that everyone on the team had to be a backup player on our special teams. Bud knew how much I hated doing that. He never gave me the assignment and let me stay home and miss that part of the practice sessions.

"Many years later, I had the opportunity to ask him why he let me stay away from the special teams practices. Bud told me that he knew how much I hated special teams work and that he also knew if he left me off the team and away from the practices, I would give him everything I had at my own position. He was right, because I did. He just simply understood me," recalls Rashad. "We had a great relationship. Our great Hall of Famer, offensive tackle Ron Yary, used to call me the teacher's pet."

Rashad had a great career in college and professional football. He attended the University of Oregon and played the wide receiver position as a sophomore before being switched to a running back, at which he became an All-American in 1971. He was subsequently elected to the College Football Hall of Fame in 2007.

His play in college was outstanding, and he was rated one of the top running backs in the nation. During the 1972 NFL Draft, Rashad was taken as the fourth overall pick in the first round by the St. Louis Cardinals, where he played for two years before going to the Buffalo Bills in 1974, the Seattle Seahawks for a short time in 1976, and then to the Vikings that same year. He remained in Minnesota until 1982.

Rashad caught 495 career passes and accumulated 44 touchdowns during his career. He was a Pro Bowl selection four times and a Second-Team All-Pro in 1979. He was a two-time First-Team All-Conference selection, a three-time Second-Team All-Conference selection, and a Most Valuable Player in the Pro Bowl in 1979.

After football Ahmad has been involved in many things. "I have lots of interests and lots of friends," he says. "I am truly enjoying life with a passion. I love taking my daughter to school every day and picking her up. It is one of my life's highlights to be there for her."

Rashad has enjoyed a long career in television broadcasting and is the executive producer for six NBA specials a year that highlight NBA players on and off the court. "It's a chance for fans to see who these players really are as individuals and not just basketball players," says Rashad.

Speaking about the Vikings 50, he says, "It was a great feeling for me. It was such a fantastic brotherhood of players being on those great teams. It was a true family atmosphere. I talk to Fran Tarkenton regularly, and we always speak about our great teammates. To be one of the 50 greatest for me is pure icing on the cake. It can't get any better than that."

A final note: For many years, most fans have thought that head coach Bud Grant mispronounced Ahmad's first name—Bud *always* called him Akmad (äk·mäd). The correct pronunciation for *Ahmad* is just that. It seems that many years back, Bud asked Ahmad how to correctly pronounce his name. Grant may in fact be the only one in professional football who pronounces it correctly.

Whether it be the famous Kramer-to-Rashad Hail Mary pass or simply his wonderful productive years as a wide receiver, it doesn't matter, because Ahmad Rashad will always be recognized as one of the 50 greatest Vikings ever.

Rashad has found success off the field, in the media. *Photo courtesy of Ahmad Rashad*

Sharockman takes down a 49ers receiver during game action.

Ed SHAROCKMAN

#45 | Defensive Back, 1961–72

When people speak of former outstanding defensive back Ed Sharockman of the Minnesota Vikings, the inevitable word is *toughness.* "He was as tough as nails and a good tackler," says former Vikings tight end Stu Voigt. "He worked hard and was always willing to pay the price. He always held his own."

Ed Sharockman grew up near the coalmines in St. Clair, Pennsylvania. "I was one of seven kids in the family, and we had a tough life growing up," says Sharockman. "I did a lot of coal picking for fuel. [My family] lived in a four-room house. We had no phone, no car, no indoor bathroom, and not much money."

Organized sports proved to be an escape from a difficult childhood. "From the time I was a kid, all I ever wanted to do was play sports," Sharockman continues. "It was my life as a youngster. In high school, I played football, basketball, and baseball. I was a quarterback on offense and a defensive back on defense."

Sharockman was an outstanding high school football player and had many offers for collegiate scholarships. "We didn't have a phone," he says, "so when recruiters called, they would have to call my aunt's house, where my grandmother also lived. They lived just down the street from us, and when they got a call for me, they would have to run down the street to get me.

"I remember one of the coaches was kind of upset because he had to wait so long on the phone for me to answer. 'What took you so long?' he hollered. 'You have got to be kidding me,' he said, when I explained [it]."

Sharockman decided to attend the University of Pittsburgh, where he starred as a cornerback for the Panthers. After his collegiate eligibility was completed, he was drafted by the Minnesota Vikings in the fifth round of the 1961 National Football League Draft and in the 22nd round of the American Football League Draft by the Dallas Texans. He chose the Vikings but missed all but one game of

> **"'Bozo', we called him. He was a tough guy who had his nose broken so many times...as tough a player as they come."**
>
> —GARY LARSEN

his rookie season after suffering a broken leg in the College All-Star Game.

"I loved playing for the Vikings," says Sharockman. "We came so close and had so many outstanding teams. We started out on the bottom as an expansion team in the early 1960s and moved our way up. By the time we got to the late 1960s, we had a great team."

Echoing seemingly universal praise for his coach, Sharockman says, "I loved playing for Bud Grant. He was a great coach and let you do your job."

Ed played for 12 seasons in the NFL—all of them with the Vikings. He finished his career with 40 interceptions and six touchdowns. All in all, he was a solid performer, a mainstay in the Vikings' defensive backfield.

During the off-season Ed did a number of things, including selling cars and then mutual funds. He eventually went full-time in the brokerage business and then earned his real-estate license, his career for 30 years. "I truly enjoyed the real-estate business," says Sharockman. "I loved to help people out. To me, if I could make people happy, that was important to me."

Sharockman played with an evident love for the game.

88

In 1962, Sharockman showed off his speed as a defensive back when he returned an interception for 88 yards downfield. (The sprint was the longest in the NFL that season, too.)

"Today in my life, I say glory to God and thank him for everything I have ever had in my life," says Ed. "He...has sent me in a new direction. I have a great outlook on life and enjoy every moment that I can spend with my family.

"I was totally surprised and humbled greatly by the selection [to the 50 greatest Vikings roll]," says Ed. "It means a great deal to me, and I sure wonder whether I deserve the honor with so many great players who played for the Vikings."

> **"For as tough a guy as he is, he is really a nice guy."**
>
> —ALAN PAGE

Reflecting on his career, he shares one anecdote. One day Ed Sharockman was having lunch with a friend, who was telling him about the difficulty he had in his job. Ed, in a concerned manner, replied, "Wow, you really had a tough job!" His friend replied, "Ed, let me tell you something. When I made a mistake I could usually fix it quickly. It might take a little time, but I could usually solve the problem or correct my mistake. When you made a mistake, you did it in front of 50,000 screaming fans, and it cost your team a touchdown. *You* are the one who had the tough job!"

And he did the tough job so well, without complaint. And considering the esteemed careers he has had in football and the private sector, Sharockman's toughness has indeed served him well.

An early photo of the Sharockman family. *Photo courtesy of Ed Sharockman*

Jeff SIEMON

#50 | Linebacker, 1972–82

Jeff Siemon is a quiet and reserved man who has devoted most of his life to ministry work. You would never know by talking to him that he was one of the fiercest middle linebackers to ever play the game. He roamed behind the line of scrimmage for the Minnesota Vikings for more than a decade, destroying running backs, blockers, and anyone else in his way. He was unequivocally one tremendous football player.

Siemon grew up in Bakersfield, California, after being born in Rochester, Minnesota (his father was a doctor at the Mayo Clinic before the family relocated to California). Jeff was one of five children in the family.

He was actively involved in sports throughout his early life, though in those early years, his first love was baseball. "I also loved to fish when I was younger, and we did a lot of fishing in Canada," recalls Siemon. "In high school I played football, basketball, and baseball and was heavily recruited by several colleges and universities. It was the same high school that former New York Giants star Frank Gifford attended. There is a tremendous history at the school for athletics." He was named as the best high school senior player on the West Coast, earning the Pop Warner Award.

Jeff chose Stanford University for his collegiate career. He was a star linebacker for Stanford and played on two Rose Bowl teams. He was given the silver anniversary Dick Butkus Award as the nation's best linebacker retroactively. In 2006, he was rewarded for his collegiate efforts by being inducted into the College Football Hall of Fame.

"I was a history major in college," says Siemon. "I liked to write and basically took liberal arts–type courses. I was particularly interested in Reformation history and developed a personal relationship with Christ. At the same time

> **"Jeff Siemon is the consummate professional and one of the best linebackers to ever play the game. His work ethic was absolutely tremendous. And above it all, he is one of the nicest guys you would ever want to meet. I love Jeff Siemon!"**
>
> —AHMAD RASHAD

Siemon takes the field.

Siemon zeroes in on the Saints' passer.

11

A ranging linebacker, Siemon seemed to cover the entire field. He retired with a career 11 fumble recoveries.

in my life, I had a real desire to someday play in the National Football League. I had spent a lot of time thinking about it because I had been very successful at the high school and collegiate levels.

"Although playing in the National Football League was a dream, I never really thought it was possible. And then I made it, and it was a great experience. Especially gratifying was having the privilege of playing football for Bud Grant. Bud was a terrific coach and a very bright man about football and about life. Bud never missed a thing. He was always aware of what was going on around him, in the game and with people. I loved playing for Bud."

Siemon was drafted by the Minnesota Vikings in the first round of the 1972 NFL Draft. He was the 10th pick overall. He turned out to be a wonderful player for 11 straight seasons with the Purple. He played in four Pro Bowls and in three Super Bowls. During his best years with the Vikings, he played alongside other linebackers Matt Blair, Roy Winston, and Wally Hilgenberg, all members of the 50 greatest Vikings in their own right.

Jeff's education continued after football, and he graduated from Simon Greenleaf School of Law. He achieved a master's degree in Christian Apologetics in 1984 and eventually began his life's work with Minnesota Search Ministries.

Christian apologetics in part presents the rationale for the Christian faith and defends the faith against objections, while it exposes the flaws of other worldviews. "This fit right in with my commitment to Christ," says Siemon. "Even while with the Vikings, I never got far from this life, as I was the team chapel coordinator on Saturday nights.

"I heard about Search Ministries through a friend, attended a conference, and met some great people. It has been my football afterlife for the past 26 years," says Jeff. "In my spare time, I love to spend time with my family, and I also love to read. I'm very interested in history, particularly military history and theology."

Siemon has built a solid reputation for himself in a lifetime that has included football and the daily practice of his faith. He is admired and respected by his former teammates and many friends and family.

In some respects, it is somewhat of an oddity that a man of such profound faith would also develop a reputation as a hard-hitting, dominating middle linebacker in professional football. But in many ways the virtues of commitment, faith, and cooperation serve him well in both vocations.

Dawn and Jeff Siemon sport the Vikings colors in the 1970s.
Photo courtesy of Jeff Siemon

Robert SMITH

#26/#20 | Running Back, 1993–2000

Robert Smith was a premier running back for the Minnesota Vikings. In many ways he played his position in a style similar to that of Ahmad Rashad. At least, in the sense that they were both pure poetry in motion. Smith's seemingly effortless running style was a pleasure to watch; he seemed to glide along through the defenses into the open field. And once he achieved that, it was a pure thrill to watch him run.

Robert Smith was a little different from some of the rest. He is a complex man, a deep thinker, and he surprised fans and teammates alike when he decided to retire from a game that appeared so easy for him to play. He is a man who is unafraid to express his opinion. He has taken tough and sometimes controversial positions on various things and is not afraid to state how he feels or what matters to him. A complicated man and accomplished scholar, he was a football player par excellence.

Smith was born in Euclid, Ohio, and grew up in the Cleveland area. "I started participating in football and track around the sixth grade," recalls Smith. "But I was also very enthused about other things besides sports. I was very interested in science and enjoyed learning everything I could…

"I was heavily recruited while I was in high school, but I wanted to stay fairly close to home so my mother would be able to see me play football. I settled on Ohio State."

Smith had an outstanding football career for the Buckeyes, but it wasn't all wine and roses. In fact, it started with a controversial decision—he quit the team after a disagreement with an assistant coach. The coach wanted Smith to skip two classes to attend practice. Smith's academic principles prevailed. He knew what he had to do, took a stand about it, and quit the Ohio State football team. He returned to the squad later, his principles intact.

After playing football for Ohio State, Smith was drafted by the Minnesota Vikings in the first round of the 1993 NFL Draft. He played for Minnesota from 1993 to 2000, retiring at a time many thought was the prime of his career. Indeed,

"Robert was a great running back and a smart football player. I was really surprised when he retired so early in his career."

—JERRY BURNS

Robert Smith doing what he does best.

Smith waves to fans during the Vikings 50 halftime ceremony.

he was inarguably one of the premier running backs in the NFL at the time.

But Smith knew. He was a person who made solid decisions, and injuries and overall health played a part in the decision. He wanted to have a career and life after football, and he wanted walking to be a part of it.

6,818
Despite what many call an abbreviated career, Robert Smith tops the Vikings leaderboards as the team's best rusher, with 6,818 yards.

During his Vikings career, Robert rushed for 6,818 yards—a 4.8-yard average—and he scored 32 touchdowns. He also was on the receiving end of 178 pass receptions, six of them touchdowns. He was twice selected to the Pro Bowl and was a one-time Second-Team All-Pro selection. In addition, he was the NFL Alumni Running Back of the Year in 2000.

His very best year in professional football came in his final season, 2000, when he rushed for 1,521 yards and led the NFC in rushing. During eight years carrying the football and catching passes, he fumbled the ball only nine times. He also set the NFL record for average yards per touchdown run, which was etched into the record books at 27.2 yards.

After he retired from football to pursue other interests such as medicine, Smith kept out of the spotlight. He was and remains a private person, though he has developed some national attention through his work with college sports broadcasting. He began in 2007 as a regular broadcaster for college football with ESPN.

In 2004, Smith wrote a book titled *The Rest of the Iceberg: An Insider's View on the World of Sport and Celebrity*. The book focuses on his personal background, his time in collegiate and professional sports with Ohio State, his career with the Minnesota Vikings, and the reasons for his retirement.

He also writes candidly on the public's obsession with sports stardom. "On the nation's obsession with football: If people would spend as much time investigating and looking at our government or some of the decisions that are made in our country as they do memorizing stats of players, we'd have a better understanding of the world and be capable of making better decisions." Strong words for a man who reached the pinnacle of success in professional football.

"I was treated well with the Vikings," says Smith. "I sincerely do miss the people in Minnesota. They are exceptionally nice people in the Midwest.... The area is a beautiful place to live, and I miss that also. I come back probably once a year or so and really enjoy my returns."

He ranks with the best who ever played for the Minnesota Vikings. He didn't really fit the style of Bill "Boom Boom" Brown or Dave Osborn and their punishing, bone-crushing, and bruising marches down the field. He didn't weave, spin, and juke like Chuck Foreman. Smith's highstep stride and fluid motions made him exciting to watch, and yet one might imagine whether he could have also excelled at the ballet or on stage. He was that type of runner and personality—somewhat distant and refined, a runner with grace and fluidity.

Fans are only sorry we couldn't enjoy him for longer.

Smith smiles during game action in 1999.

Studwell rallies teammates to get ready for play.

Scott STUDWELL

#55 | Linebacker, 1977–90

When Scott Studwell was drafted by the Minnesota Vikings in the ninth round of the National Football League's 1977 Player Draft, hardly anyone thought that he would become the player that he was—let alone remain a major part of the Minnesota Vikings organization some 30 years later. Studwell was a stalwart linebacker for the Purple for 14 years, and he has stayed on with the team in the front office for the past 21 seasons, currently serving as the director of college scouting.

Studwell describes his humble beginnings in Evansville, Indiana. "I grew up in a river town with an older brother—who was a better athlete than me—and two sisters. My parents were very athletic, and my dad played college football at Wesleyan College. We were a middle-class family, and my dad ran an insurance agency.

"Sports were big for me as a kid," recalls Studwell. "My true love was with baseball. It was my favorite." Even so, he was truly a born outdoorsman. "One of my real passions was fishing. I loved to fish the country ponds. Every summer we went out East to the beach and spent a lot of time on Fire Island.

"I spent so much time outside as a youngster that I didn't get very exposed to professional football," remembers Scott. "I wasn't real big…before high school, and I recall around the eighth grade I was 5'2" and weighed 110 pounds. But I grew fast—about a foot—and gained a lot of weight [by the time I got to high school]. I was a quarterback, running back, and a linebacker on defense."

Studwell started college at the University of Illinois in 1972, and at the time, freshmen were not eligible to play. Standing on the sideline only lit a fire in him; he was ready to go. By the following year, he started as a defensive tackle for the Illini, was switched to defensive end, and ultimately ended up at linebacker.

When he reached his senior year at Illinois, he had become an exceptional player—and he was getting some feelers from the professional teams. And little wonder; he was a crushing linebacker who had led the Big Ten conference in total tackles.

"When the Vikings took me in the ninth round of the player draft, I was really disappointed," Studwell remembers. "I sincerely thought I would be taken in the earlier rounds. All I concentrated on was football. I didn't work in the off-season, I just trained to be ready for the season to begin.

"I spent a lot of time lifting weights and had started the weights routine back in high school. I loved the game and

"He was always excited. I remember how he would really hit you hard and then laugh at you. He was a solid leader of the defense."

—GARY ZIMMERMAN

4

In 1986, Studwell recovered a career-best four fumbles. He would go on to wrap up 16 in his career.

could not believe that a person could actually get paid to do something they loved to do. It was unbelievable!"

Despite any perceived slight, he had met his goal. He was getting paid to do something he loved—and truly earning his paychecks. Scott played for 14 years in the NFL as a middle linebacker. During his esteemed career, he played in the Pro Bowl twice and was All-Pro three times and played in 201 games as a Viking. He also owns the NFL record for recording more tackles with a single team than any other player in the history of the NFL.

On November 29, 2009, Scott was inducted into the Vikings Ring of Honor. He is the team leader in combined tackles with 1,981, single-season tackles with 230 in 1981, and single-game tackles, which he accomplished in 1985 when he tackled Detroit Lions players 24 times in one afternoon. He was also named to the Vikings 25th and 40th Anniversary Teams.

After a long career on the gridiron, Studwell began to sense it was time to give up the game he loved. "My last season, I got hurt and began to realize that it was time to call it quits. But I really miss the game and every aspect of it. I would play tomorrow if I could," he says.

"When I retired, I didn't know what to do. I had gone to school to play football, and [then] it was over," he continues. "In 1991, I knew that I wanted to find a way to stay active in the game. Roger Hedrick, Vikings team president, found the way for me, and I'm still here as the director of college scouting.

"I have a great career in the Vikings front office," says Scott. "I love to evaluate talent—to look at a player's character, their intelligence, their passion, and their work ethic. Unfortunately, there is not a way to measure the size of their heart. And because of that, we do miss a few.

"During the season, I am on the road most of the time, but in the summer I get some time to spend with my family at our lake home in Wisconsin. It is there I can get back to my passion for fishing," says Scott.

From one small pond to a much, much larger one, Studwell has taken everything that has come to him in stride. Studwell continues to be a respected and deeply committed member of the Minnesota Vikings organization. He is a winner who wants to win every Sunday. Scott has earned just about every honor and recognition that a player would strive to earn. He played the game—and he played it to his fullest every minute of his life.

"Scott always played the game hard at practice and during games for the Vikings. He was a tremendous linebacker and was a Hall of Fame–caliber player."

—JERRY BURNS

When Studwell was named to the list of the 50 greatest Vikings, he was surprised and honored. "I tried not to think about it while the process was going on," says Scott. "Now to know that I made the 50 greatest, the honor is wonderful. I am part of a team with some great players. It was more than I could have ever hoped for in my career in professional football."

The Studwell family takes in a Vikings game.
Photo courtesy of Scott Studwell

Doug SUTHERLAND

#69 | Defensive Tackle, 1971–80

When Gary Larsen retired in 1974, the Purple People Eaters were short a defensive lineman. Could the team recapture the magic that the fearsome foursome unleashed on their opponents without Larsen? With the emergence of Doug Sutherland, a 6'3", 250-pound bruiser formerly of the New Orleans Saints, the answer was a resounding *yes*.

Sutherland became a mainstay of the Vikings' defensive line, playing alongside Jim Marshall, Alan Page, and Carl Eller. Joining the elite defensive fraternity, Sutherland played in three Super Bowls for Minnesota.

Sutherland hails from Superior, Wisconsin, coincidentally the same town where former Minnesota Vikings head coach Bud Grant grew up. Sutherland played college football at the University of Wisconsin–Superior, where he was noticed by the New Orleans Saints, who selected him in the 14th round of the 1970 draft.

Sutherland looks back on his childhood with fondness. "My father was a construction worker in Superior," he says. "Growing up, I was an avid hunter and fisherman. I loved to be in the woods and on the lakes and still do today. My mother was a hunter also—and in fact, she hunted until she was about 80 years old.

"Superior is a small town on Lake Superior. I was involved in just about all sports as a kid. I was recruited heavily in high school, and I also participated in track. Eventually I ended up with some shot-put and discus records."

Sutherland was a defensive tackle at the time he was drafted by the New Orleans Saints, but they didn't know quite what to do with him. He played as a defensive lineman in training camp, but by the time the regular season started, he was at the middle linebacker spot for the first three games and then found himself as an offensive guard by the fourth week of the regular season.

"When I was traded to the Vikings the following season, I came to them as an offensive guard," he recalls. "I always looked at the trade as going from the outhouse to

"Doug Sutherland was one of our outstanding defensive linemen. He was very reliable...an extremely hard worker [who] worked his way into the starting lineup."

—STU VOIGT

Sutherland in the
middle of the action.

Sutherland takes
care of business.

the penthouse. The Vikings had been to the Super Bowl and were developing into a great football team.

"After joining the Vikings as an offensive guard, middle linebacker Lonnie Warwick got hurt, and I was moved to the middle linebacker position," he remembers. "In 1972, Fran Tarkenton was traded back to the Vikings, and I was a defensive tackle again. With Fran and the other great players, we became a dominant team in the NFL for many years."

When asked whether he had considered professional football as a long-term career goal, Sutherland is humble. "I never really thought I had a chance to make it in the National Football League. I loved the game and had a great opportunity with the Vikings. One of the things I feel the best about is being a part of the famous line known as the Purple People Eaters. And when it came to naming the team's 50 greatest Vikings, we all made the team. That was a tremendous feeling," he says.

After football, Sutherland pursued a few jobs in sales before settling into his current career; since 1989, he has been in real estate. "The real-estate business is something I have been really interested in, and I have sincerely enjoyed [it]," he says.

And of course he still fishes and hunts now and again. "[It's] one of my greatest passions.... I especially enjoy bow hunting."

Reflecting on a 12-year football career, Sutherland shows gratitude. Like many others, he shows affection and respect for Bud Grant, the coach and "molder of men." "I was very fortunate to be able to spend most of my career with the Minnesota Vikings, and I really enjoyed playing for Bud Grant. I learned about how to manage people from Bud. One of the things he taught me was to get out of my employees' way in the real-estate business and let them work. He was a tremendous manager of people, and just watching him taught me a great deal."

Doug Sutherland was a solid football player for the Minnesota Vikings for 10 years, perhaps the greatest decade in Vikings history. He was well liked by his teammates and versatile enough to have played the game of football at the highest level as a middle linebacker, offensive guard, and defensive tackle. He will forever be associated with that most elite of defensive units, the Purple People Eaters. It doesn't get much better than that.

Sutherland loved playing for coach Bud Grant.

3
Automatic at defensive tackle, Doug Sutherland played in three Super Bowls with the Vikings.

No. 10 celebrates six.

Fran
TARKENTON

#10 | Quarterback, 1961–66, 1972–78

When fans think of the greatest Vikings of all time, the men who shaped the team's excellence, who wore the Purple proudly and victoriously over the decades, they must begin with Fran Tarkenton. Without a doubt, he is one of the greatest quarterbacks and playmakers in the history of the game and perhaps the most exciting player to ever step onto a football field.

In 1961, the newly minted Minnesota Vikings got set to play the Chicago Bears at Metropolitan Stadium in Bloomington, Minnesota; it was the franchise's first-ever regular-season game. The Vikings were a mishmash of players who other teams had given up on and greener-than-green rookies who knew little about the game of professional football. Their head coach had never coached a game in his life.

The Bears, on the other hand, were one of the most feared teams in the NFL. Led by legendary coach George Halas, they were the Monsters of the Midway. Just a couple of weeks earlier, in a preseason game, the Bears had decimated the Vikings. Suffice it to say, the Bears were *heavy* favorites.

But on this day, a young rookie quarterback by the name of Francis Asbury Tarkenton came off the bench early in the first quarter, and before he was finished he had thrown four touchdown passes and run for another. On this day, the upstart Vikings defeated the mighty Bears 37–13, in what many have called the greatest upset in the history of the National Football League.

Francis Tarkenton was born the son of a preacher in Athens, Georgia. As a youngster, he starred in football, basketball, and baseball at Athens High School. He went on to attend the University of Georgia, where he was an exceptional quarterback for the Bulldogs, leading the team to the Southeastern Conference championship. For his stellar play at the collegiate level, Tarkenton was inducted into the Georgia Sports Hall of Fame in 1977, the College

"He is 'Fran the Man,' no doubt about that. Fran is one of a kind. He was a great quarterback for us, very smart and really knew defenses. He truly understood the game."

—MICK TINGELHOFF

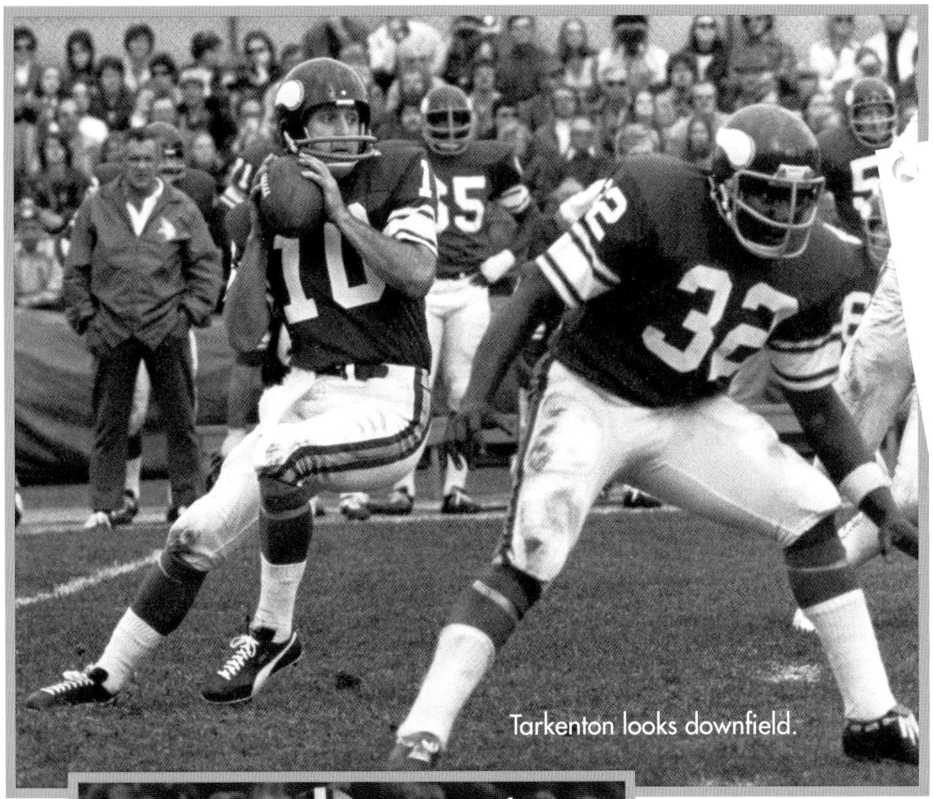

Tarkenton looks downfield.

300

One of the most prolific passers of his time, Fran Tarkenton was the first QB to throw 300 career touchdown passes, among many other NFL hallmarks.

Confirming the first down.

Football Hall of Fame in 1987, and (for his career in football) the Athens Athletic Hall of Fame in 2000.

Tarkenton was drafted by the Minnesota Vikings in the third round of the 1961 NFL Draft, the team's first; he was the 29th overall pick. "When they pick you that low in the draft as a quarterback, they don't think you can play," says Tarkenton. "But I never had a doubt. I knew I could make the plays and never doubted my abilities to be successful in the National Football League."

He was right. In his 13 years with the Vikings from 1961 to 1966 and again from 1972 to 1978, Tarkenton led the Purple to three Super Bowls. He was selected to nine Pro Bowls and was a two-time All-Pro selection, a one-time Second-Team All-Pro selection, and was named the Most Valuable Player in the NFL in 1964 and 1975. He took the Vikings to three NFC championships, was the 1975 NFL Offensive Player of the Year, the 1975 UPI NFC Player of the Year, and took home the Bert Bell Award that year, too.

His No. 10 has been retired by the Vikings. He was named to the team's 25th Anniversary Team, the 40th Anniversary Team, and the Ring of Honor. He was also inducted into the Pro Football Hall of Fame in 1986.

Tarkenton is the all-time Vikings career passing leader, with 33,098 yards. He threw for 239 touchdowns for the team, also a franchise best. He tops scores of categories on the team leaderboards. There is no denying the legacy he has left with the Minnesota Vikings.

But Fran Tarkenton is not just about football, and he never has been. He is a devoted family man who never gives life a rest. He brings a positive enthusiasm to every single day, radiates it to anyone near him. There is little question why he has been successful on the gridiron, in his many businesses, and in life. He has a work ethic and a commitment to excellence second to none.

"I'll never quit working," says Tarkenton. "What would I do? Every day I look forward to tomorrow and the next day and the next. I enjoy every minute."

Of all of Tarkenton's experiences on the gridiron, there is perhaps one element that has enriched his life more than the rest. He credits coach Bud Grant with giving him a real life's education. "Bud Grant has more common sense than any man I have ever known," says Tarkenton. "Grant is simply the type of guy who has it figured out. He possesses a shrewd understanding of people and the way things should be better than anyone. He is a magnificent student of others and a great manager."

Fran Tarkenton has now been a businessman for many years. He has started numerous ventures and is a national spokesman for the small-business owner and entrepreneur on many national radio and television networks. He is known to speak his mind and defend his principles. He is driven, confident, passionate, and a leader.

Looking back on 50 years of Minnesota Vikings football, there are plenty of great moments to choose from. The old days fill the hearts of the Purple faithful. Stopping to reflect on the franchise's foundation, we see Bud Grant on the sideline in his familiar pose, with his cap and headset on; Bill "Boom Boom" Brown crashing through the line; and the Osborns, Voigts, Pages, Ellers, Marshalls, Tingelhoffs, and so many others clad in the Purple. And right there in the middle of it all is the quarterback from Georgia, No. 10, Fran Tarkenton, leading the parade as one of the 50 greatest Vikings of all time.

Tarkenton is as passionate about his life in business as he was on the field of play.
Photo courtesy of Fran Tarkenton

Henry THOMAS

#97 | Defensive Tackle, 1987–94

Henry Thomas was literally in the center of all the action on Sunday afternoons in the National Football League. He was a nose tackle on some very tough Vikings teams. He was on the top, the bottom, and in the middle of all the pileups. He was hit from above, below, and both sides, likely on every single play. Everywhere he looked there were 300-pound football players trying to move him out of the way, sandwich him, or bury him in a mass of bodies. Still, with all the mayhem going on around him, he managed to get to the quarterback and sack him to the ground 93.5 times.

Henry Thomas grew up in Houston, Texas. "I was a quiet kid," he remembers, "but I had a lot of fun as a youngster. I was involved in a lot of sports…and we were always playing some kind of pickup game…

"I started playing baseball when I was about 10 years old. I was a big kid and loved the game, but once I saw a few curveballs later on, I was out of there. No more of that sport for me," he says, laughing.

"My friends all thought I should get into football as a youngster, but my mom was against it. She did not want me to play. I had to forge a [parent's signature] on the signup document in order to play. I had to save my money in order to be on the team, and I remember it took me about four months to gather what I needed.

"My mom eventually found out I was playing and came to one of my games but left after the first quarter. By the time I was playing in high school, she was into it. In high school, I was playing just about every position."

Henry was recruited heavily out of high school and settled on Louisiana State University, where he became one of the school's greatest defensive linemen. Thomas credits LSU with much of his football education. "I learned a lot

"Henry was a very underrated player. He allowed others on the team to do well because of the way he played. Keith Millard, John Randle, and I were able to succeed because of Henry Thomas."

—CHRIS DOLEMAN

Henry Thomas catches the Cardinals' Tom Tupa for a sack.

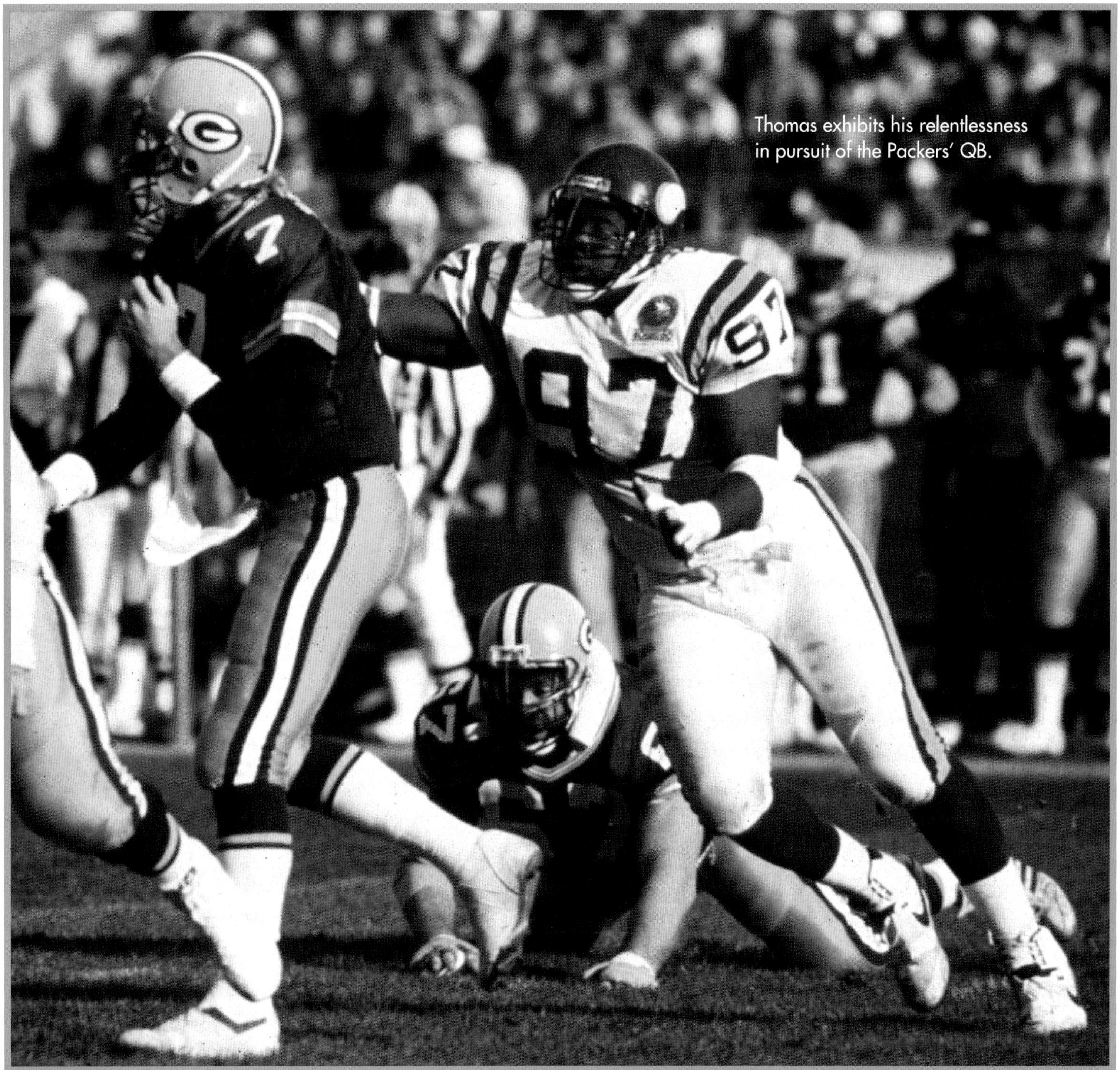

Thomas exhibits his relentlessness in pursuit of the Packers' QB.

"Henry Thomas is a great person and a wonderful friend of mine. He was an extremely smart football player, very talented, and a technician of the game. He could really play."

—CARL LEE

[about] technique and how to play the game at LSU. The coaches there were really outstanding."

He was drafted by the Minnesota Vikings in the third round, 72nd overall, of the 1987 NFL Draft. He played for the Vikings from 1987 to 1994 before finishing out his career with Detroit and New England. He recorded more than 1,000 tackles in his 14-year career in the NFL and scored four touchdowns—not bad for a defensive tackle in the league.

Reflecting on his years in Purple, Thomas says, "I loved my years with the Vikings, and I really enjoyed playing for Jerry Burns. The best part of it was all the great friends that I made on the team. Every Thursday night our defensive line would get together. Keith Millard, Al Noga, Chris Doleman, Doug Martin, John Randle—we were a very close bunch of guys. Those are ...great memories of my years in Minnesota.

"When I found out that I was named one of the 50 greatest Vikings, I was deeply honored. To be named along with the greats of the past like Alan Page, Jim Marshall, Carl Eller, and so many others—to be just mentioned with them is really something."

Now retired from professional football, Thomas is a proud father of his four daughters. "I love to play golf, do a little betting on the ponies, and also like to bowl, but most of all, I love being a dad to my daughters," he says.

Sometimes the urge to get back into football hits Henry. He did a coaching internship with the Vikings recently (he also did one previously with the Indianapolis Colts), so he may well find himself back in the ranks at some point. Either way, his legacy in the game—and with the Minnesota Vikings—is a sure thing.

93.5

Thomas' 93.5 sacks testify to his tenacity at the defensive end position.

The Thomas family.
Photo courtesy of Henry Thomas

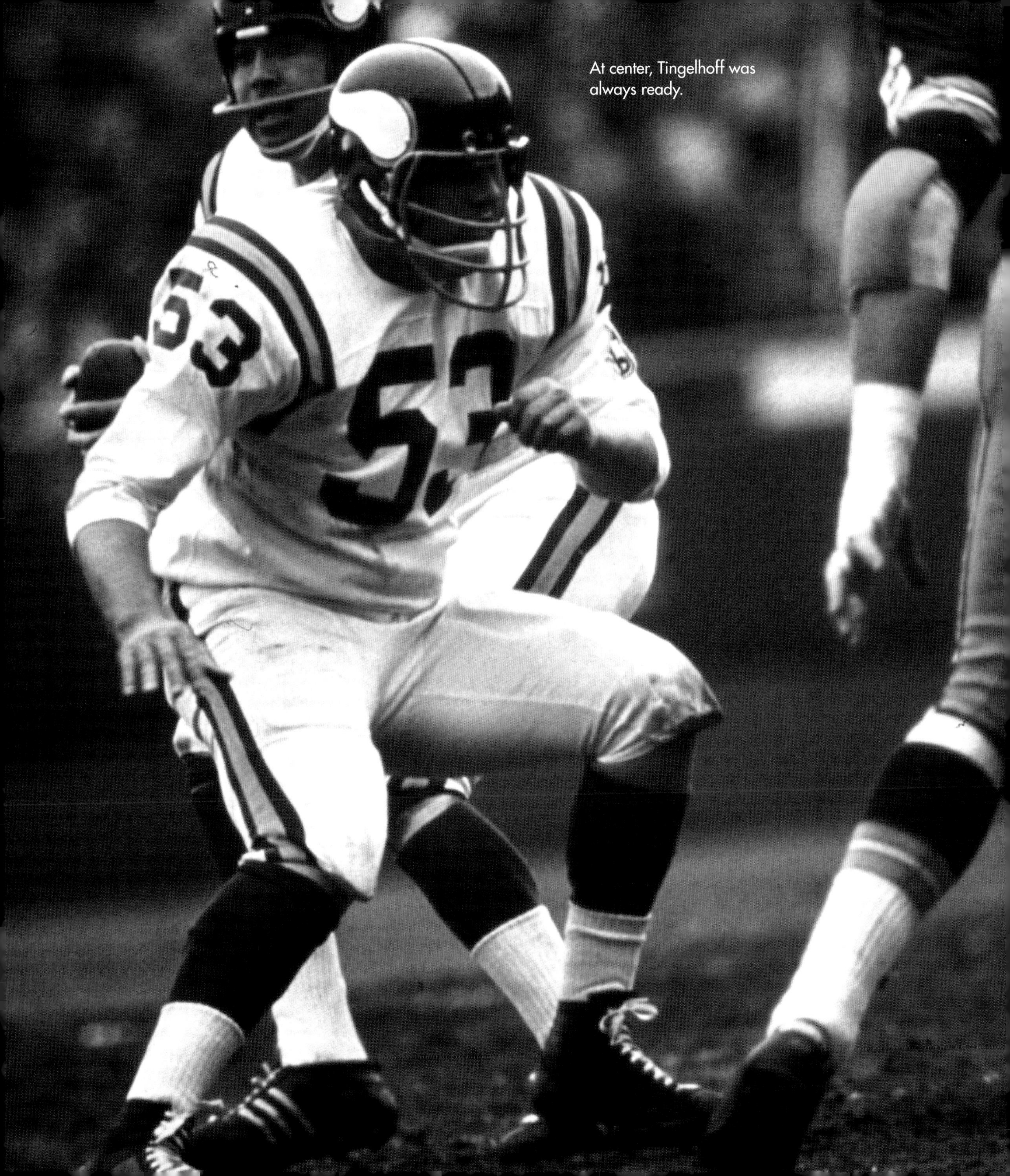

At center, Tingelhoff was always ready.

Mick TINGELHOFF

#53 | Center, 1962–78

He was just a farm kid from Nebraska. No one in the professional ranks thought he was a good enough player to select him in the 1962 NFL Draft. It took a visit from then–Minnesota Vikings head coach Norm Van Brocklin to get Mick to come to Minnesota. He signed with the Vikings as a free agent, and the rest was history. He started at center for the Vikings for the next 17 years. And during all of that time, he never missed a game.

Former Vikings center Godfrey Zaunbrecher had one of the most memorable and honest lines imaginable about the great Vikings center: "I am the third team center on a football team that has only two centers on the roster. I play behind Mick Tingelhoff and Mick Tingelhoff hurt."

Tingelhoff and Fran Tarkenton were longtime teammates and have been close friends for many years. In his autobiography, *Every Day Is Game Day*, Tarkenton writes almost reverently about his beloved center. "Mick Tingelhoff was as tough a player as any who ever played. If I gathered every football player that I knew or played with in my life and put them all in a room with the instructions to fight their way out, I would put my money on Mick to get there first.

"He was absolutely ferocious as a blocker and pass protector. He even snapped the ball for punts, field goals, and extra points. If they kept the records for how many tackles he made after interceptions and on punts, his numbers would be staggering.... On the field when I was scrambling, Mick made some of the most devastating blocks imaginable. He took people out of plays—and sometimes out of games. He would make tough hits, clean hits that were absolutely shocking to watch.

"The fact that he is not enshrined in the Pro Football Hall of Fame is a major disservice to the game. He played for 17 years and never missed a game. He went to six Pro

"Mick was the undisputed leader of the Vikings with Jim Marshall for years and years.... Mick held his own with some of the game's best, Ray Nitschke, Mike Lucci, and Dick Butkus."

—STU VOIGT

"Mick Tingelhoff was as durable as they come. He never missed a game. He was an extremely hard worker and full of determination."

—DAVE OSBORN

Tingelhoff was a Viking through and through.

240

Tingelhoff's 240 consecutive starts are an NFL record for centers.

Bowls, four Super Bowls, and played on plenty of championship teams."

Tarkenton and Tingelhoff have been friends for decades, and the two have a good time teasing each other. Mick used to say, "I never worried too much if I missed my block when Fran was scrambling around the field; I would just wait for a while, and my man would be back again."

Mick Tingelhoff was born on a farm and grew up in Lexington, Nebraska, a small town near the middle of the state. "I had to walk about a mile and a half to school every day," remembers Tingelhoff. "As kids, we were always involved in doing our chores around the farm. I remember how we had to milk the cows by hand, long before the milking machines. We didn't have electricity until I was in about the eighth grade.

"One day around the ninth grade, my history teacher, Merle Appleby, grabbed me by the neck and told me to get out for football. I did and wound up getting a scholarship to go to Nebraska. It's really the only place I wanted to go." While in high school, Tingelhoff earned honors as a high school All-American, All-State, and All-Conference center.

At Nebraska, Tingelhoff earned three letters in football and was cocaptain of the Cornhuskers his senior year. He played in the Senior Bowl and the All-American Bowl and is a member of the Nebraska Football Hall of Fame.

After joining the Minnesota Vikings, Mick soon became the starting center and never left. He was a six-time Pro Bowl selection, a five-time Associated Press First-Team All-Pro selection, an AP Second-Team All-Pro selection, and an AP First-Team All-NFC selection. In 1969, he was named the NFL's Top Offensive Lineman of the Year.

The Vikings retired Tingelhoff's No. 53. He is enshrined in the team's Ring of Honor, too.

But the Ring of Honor isn't the only esteemed company with whom Tingelhoff is associated. He is also one of the 10 Vikings players who played in all four Super Bowls. When he retired, teammate Jim Marshall and he stood atop the NFL record books for consecutive games started. Interestingly, the only player to eclipse their record in the following decades has been onetime Viking Brett Favre.

Tingelhoff's post-football career has been varied, but one thing has been a constant: he remains closely involved in Vikings alumni functions. Like many of his former teammates, he enjoys hunting and fishing and is an avid outdoorsman.

In August 2011, he was named the recipient of the President Gerald R. Ford Legends Award. The award is given, according to the foundation, to men who have "played the center position at the collegiate or professional level, made extraordinary contributions to his team during his football career, or have proven to be an exemplary citizen, philanthropist, or leader in the business of football community."

When longtime Minnesota Vikings loyalists and faithful followers look back at the history of the Purple and think of the great teams and great players of the past, one figure stands in a hunched-over position as the linchpin and solid anchor of the rest. No matter what the situation, the conditions, or location, when the Vikings took the field, Mick Tingelhoff was the starting center. He seemed to be there forever. He almost was.

In the hearts and minds of those who know by watching and remembering the great center, there is a spot waiting for him in the Pro Football Hall of Fame. Until then and forever after, he will always be one of the 50 greatest Vikings.

Tingelhoff shows off one of the fringe benefits of playing in the Land of 10,000 Lakes.
Photo courtesy of Mick Tingelhoff

Stu VOIGT

#83 | Tight End, 1970–80

Stu Voigt grew up near Madison, Wisconsin, where his father was the head of the Department of Natural Resources for the state of Wisconsin. "Growing up in Wisconsin, I was, of course, a Green Bay Packer fan," says Voigt. "They were our team. The Badgers were big in the state, and the Minnesota/Wisconsin rivalry was huge, and each had been to a few Rose Bowls.... And I just wanted to be a part of it all."

Looking back on his days as a student-athlete, Voigt remembers, "I played all the sports. I really enjoyed the competition.... I grew fast—growth spurts, you might say. I was about 150 pounds in the eighth grade, and by the ninth grade I was 210 pounds and 6'1". When I graduated in the spring of 1966, I thought baseball would be my sport. I was a catcher and had played well in high school," recalls Stu. "But it wasn't just sports for me. I was determined to get an education also."

Voigt's hometown roots ran deep. "I was recruited heavily in high school and had 50 scholarship offers from colleges and universities. However, there was never a doubt about where I was going to college. I loved the Wisconsin Badgers, and that is where I was going to go."

Stu had an outstanding career at Wisconsin and was sort of a triple-option player. He was a tight end and tailback in the I formation in addition to being on special teams.

Voigt was drafted by the Minnesota Vikings in the 10th round, 260th overall, of the 1970 NFL Draft. "I was disappointed [being called so late]," he remembers. "But I had a big supporter already on the Vikings in Dale Hackbart, who also went to Wisconsin.

"I remember my first trip to the Viking offices. The team had rented space in the Southtown shopping area. I came in and was kind of unprepared for where I was. I'm not sure what I thought was going to happen, but the space—well, it

"Stu was a tremendous athlete. I knew him from high school competition. He was an excellent tight end for the Vikings and could really catch the football. We used to call him 'Chainsaw.'"

—DOUG SUTHERLAND

Voigt was a great blocker and
pass receiver.

was kind of small and crowded, and I was kind of thinking, *Okay, where is the rest of it?*"

Whatever his expectations, Voigt took to the team like a duck to water, building a solid career with Minnesota as a sound blocking and receiving tight end. He was also one of quarterback Fran Tarkenton's favorite targets.

"I loved to throw the ball to Stu Voigt, our tight end," Tarkenton says. "He was a very smart and disciplined player, a dependable tight end for the Vikings for 11 years. Stu was one of my roommates for a while, and he was always fun to be around. I'd bet there was no one who enjoyed putting on a Viking uniform more than he did; he was always proud to wear the Purple colors."

Remembering those great Vikings squads, Voigt says, "The team had a swagger about them. They had learned how to win under Bud Grant and been to a recent Super Bowl. They...were a good football team. I was glad to be a part of it."

Voigt credits a lot of their success to their coach's eye. "Bud [Grant] looked for the guys who could make plays. And he found them in the Tingelhoffs, Ellers, Marshalls,

Voigt was always proud to wear the Purple.

363
Voigt had a career-best season in 1975, when he posted 363 yards per scrimmage.

Voigt looks for a seam against the Bears.

and Gary Larsens, and so many others who formed the foundation for the Vikings.

"I wanted to play a long time," recalls Stu, "but you just never knew for sure what was going to happen. I was always trying to [improve], but there was always someone around trying to take your position.

"It was so different back then from the way the NFL is now. Bud Grant was the head coach, and he had six assistant coaches—very much unlike the way it is today with so many more coaches. We had five owners, and they traveled with the team," recalls Stu. "I played for 11 years, and I had no idea who they were. But we were a family, and many of us have been friends for life ever since."

In the off-season Voigt took advantage of the downtime and went back to school to get his master's degree in business. He has been involved in many prosperous ventures since his retirement from football, including real estate and banking.

"Stu was a very intelligent player. He had excellent hands. I always told him he could catch a two-yard pass for a three-yard gain."

—JERRY BURNS

In the passing years, his loyalty to the team has only grown. He is one of the most active alumni in the community and frequently serves as an ambassador for the organization.

"It was the crown jewel for me to be named to the 50 greatest Vikings team," says Voigt. "It was really special for me. I have been very fortunate to play as long as I did. I have always been treated so well here. I truly bleed purple!"

Voigt takes to the press box with legendary broadcaster Ray Scott.

Gene Washington beats Green Bay's Ken Ellis off the block during the October 17, 1971, contest between the Vikings and Packers. *Photo courtesy of Getty Images*

Gene WASHINGTON

#84 | Wide Receiver, 1967–72

Gene Washington grew up in LaPorte, Texas, a small town of about 6,500 people. "I went to DeWalt Elementary School," says Washington. "It was an all-black school, which had grades one through eight. We didn't have much in the way of sports going on during that part of my childhood, but I can say that education and religion was very important to me.... I was always brought up to do well in school and to be respectful of people and stay out of trouble," he says.

"My dad worked for an electric company, and my mom was a maid. They worked hard. I was bussed to Baytown for high school, which was also an all-black high school," says Gene. "Everything was segregated at that time and was pretty much accepted.

"It was in the ninth grade that I started to get involved in sports. I used to get a ride home from the football coach after practice because the school buses were no longer running that late in the day. It was the same for the other sports, too, [and] the football coach, the basketball coach, and the track coach all brought me home after practices. "

In part because of the transportation arrangement, Washington formed close bonds with his high school coaches. "There was Johnny Peeples in football, Roy Hutchins in track, and Robert Strayhan in basketball. They all really meant a lot to me," says Washington, affectionately.

If high school was formative for Washington as an athlete, it was even more so as a person. "It was in the ninth grade that I met my wife, and we have been together now for 45 years," says Gene. "She was bussed also, and if it wasn't for segregation and the whole bussing to school situation, we would not have met each other."

"I competed against Gene in track while we were in college, so we knew each other before joining the Vikings. He was a big receiver with great speed and made as many big plays as anyone."

—STU VOIGT

Washington loved sports and became a big follower of Ohio State football. "Paul Warfield was a role model for me," he says. "I really looked up to him. At that time, it didn't appear that a school like Ohio State would be in my future. I was recruited by the all-black schools. I couldn't go to Texas or Rice or Southern Methodist. Everything was segregated.

"But I had a connection through the father of the legendary Bubba Smith, who went to Michigan State. He talked to the Spartans coach, Duffy Daugherty, and that's how I got connected there and ended up being offered a scholarship.

"I had a good high school career playing wide receiver, quarterback, and defense," recalls Gene. "I also ran track and was one of the best high school hurdlers in the state." In fact, it was actually Washington's track prowess that got him to Michigan State. The football team was out of scholarships for the year but were able to offer one from the track team.

"[Going] to East Lansing, it was the first time I had ever been on an airplane," recalls Gene. "I had never been in the air or in a hotel before. It was quite an experience for me. I didn't know how to order off a menu, and when we went out to eat, I just told the waitress that I would have what the coaches were having. It was very interesting and all new for me. I had lived

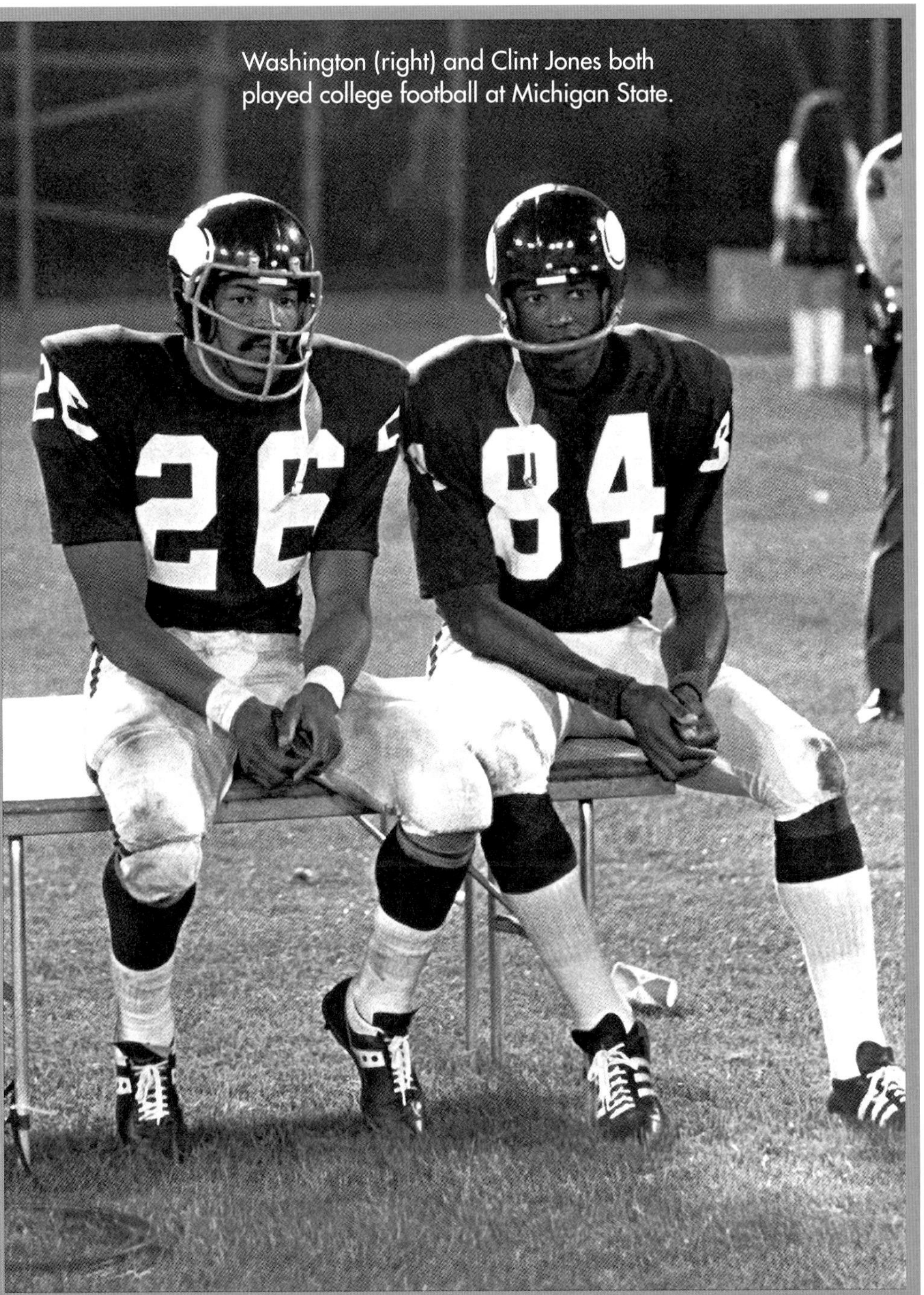

Washington (right) and Clint Jones both played college football at Michigan State.

"Gene Washington was an outstanding receiver for the Vikings. He was a tremendous deep-ball threat and a great teammate with very high standards."

—RON YARY

a life in the segregated South, and now I was called by my first name and treated real friendly. I will always remember that."

To call Washington's arrival in Michigan culture shock is a gross understatement. "When I got to Michigan State, there were more freshmen on campus than the number of people in my hometown," he recalls.

With the solid track background, Washington had extraordinary tools to develop into an excellent football player for the Spartans. By his sophomore year, he was a starter—and he never missed a game in his three years at Michigan State. Washington's exceptional play earned him an induction into the College Football Hall of Fame in 2011.

"We had a great team. In the 1967 National Football League Draft we had Bubba Smith go first in the draft, Clinton Jones as the second overall pick, George Webster went fifth, and I went eighth, all of us picked in the first round," he says.

Speaking of the Vikings' faith in him, having drafted him so high, Washington says, "I knew I had to be successful in pro football. I had nothing else to go back to." And he *was* successful. Washington played for Minnesota from 1967 to 1972, playing out his final two seasons with the Denver Broncos.

Washington's career in Purple was something special. In 1969 and 1970 he was selected to the All-Pro Team, and in 1970 and 1971, he played in the Pro Bowl. He played on four divisional championship teams and one NFL title team. He also played in one Super Bowl with the Vikings.

During the off-season Washington returned to Michigan State, where he counseled students. This led to his work in student affairs, which he pursued once his pro football career was wrapped. Parlaying his skills as an assessor of talent, he finished his professional career in human resources management.

1969

Washington's first Pro Bowl selection was in 1969, after he finished the season in the NFL's top 10 in touchdowns, receiving yards, and yards per reception.

Over the years, Washington has been the recipient of many awards and honors for football as well as his corporate and charity work.

Reflecting on his legacy, Washington speaks with pride. "From where I came from in the segregated South, it all turned out pretty well. It has been wonderful. I was really pleased when I found out I had been named to the 50 greatest Vikings team. I have been away from the game for a long time, and to be included with players like Randy Moss and the Carters is incredible."

During his playing career, Gene Washington could really run and stretch the field of play. He was a big-play receiver who was a superstar in the collegiate ranks, and he carried his prowess and fame into the pros. And for those who had the opportunity to watch the long bombs and touchdown passes to Gene Washington, there is little question about what he meant to the Vikings.

Ed WHITE

#62 | Offensive Guard, 1969–77

Ed White was a major force on the Minnesota Vikings offensive line for nine years before going on to the San Diego Chargers for another eight. Seventeen years at the heart of an offensive line in the National Football League is a remarkable feat, and in all of those years, there is no doubt he was among the very best.

White remembers his idyllic childhood in Southern California. "I grew up in the outskirts of San Diego," he says. "I was a country boy who loved being outside. We did a lot of tent camping when I was young, and I really enjoyed it.

"I played a lot of sports, but they were never really organized until I got to the high school level."

But what a high school team it was. "Six of the guys that I played with on a regular basis ended up with college scholarships, and two of us played professional football," White says, proudly.

"I was a fullback my freshman year in high school," says White. "Our family moved to the lower dessert, and I played football at Indio High School outside of Palm Springs. I loved football—every single part of the game."

White was aggressively recruited in high school by several colleges, many of them Pac-10 Conference schools. "My goal was to play on the defensive line because I hated the offensive line," says White. "It didn't matter, however what I thought, because I played offensive guard [in every game] except for my final game against Stanford, when the coach finally let me play on the defensive line." But then, and only then, because of injuries to other personnel. "I made the Pac-10 Lineman of the Week. That didn't matter either, because I was drafted by the Vikings in 1969 as an offensive guard," White continues.

While playing college football, Ed was an All-American, named to the College Football Hall of Fame, the Breitbart Hall of Fame, and the East-West Shrine Game Hall of Fame.

"Ed is a very close friend of mine. We talk all the time. He was a great football player...[who] should be in the Pro Football Hall of Fame."

—RON YARY

White keeps his Packers defender at bay.

Putting on a menacing pose.

24

They say it's all about the postseason. And with 24 playoff games played in his pro career, White ranks sixth all-time among NFL players.

As a pro, He played in 241 games, setting an NFL record for offensive linemen. He played in both the NFC and the AFC Pro Bowls with the Vikings and Chargers, respectively. He was handed All-Pro honors four times. He is enshrined in the San Diego Chargers Hall of Fame and, of course, is one of the Vikings' 50 greatest.

"I loved playing for the Vikings," says White. "There were so many of us that were together for such a long period of time. We became such a close-knit group that went out together, hunted and fished together...

"Bud Grant was our coach, and he was a very loyal person. He got a good group of players and kept them all together for a long period of time."

Despite his outstanding onfield accomplishments, it is the people who remain White's most cherished football memories. "In my 17 years in professional football, I was very fortunate to have played for only three coaches," he says. "I played for Bud Grant in Minnesota and Tommy Prothro and Don Coryell at San Diego. And I had the opportunity in my career to play alongside so many great linemen, like Mick Tingelhoff, Ron Yary, Russ Washington, and...Grady Alderman."

Beyond the gridiron, he boasted another talent: a penchant for arm wrestling. In fact, in 1975, White won the NFL Arm Wrestling Championship. "I was extremely quick in the sport and obviously very strong," he recalls. "I won some of my matches in less than a second. I used to bet people hamburgers for lunch. I got a lot of free lunches out of the competition. When you are wrestling for food, you can get pretty good at it. I started doing it in college and got pretty serious about it. Later on I won a $10,000 prize by beating six of my competitors in a total of 14 seconds."

"Ed White was a great guard and a terrific blocker."

—JERRY BURNS

In the off-season, White worked for a landscape and architecture company, where he labored to find jobs for disadvantaged kids. After his retirement from the NFL, he began working in the coaching ranks. He coached six years at the college level and eight years in the pros.

Now retired from coaching, he devotes his life to his family and his artwork. He has been commissioned to create numerous bronze sculptures, many of them sports-related and most in private collections. He is also an accomplished painter.

White is the executive director of the nonprofit Oak Lake Art Center. A percentage of his profits from the sale of his own art goes to the foundation as well, which supports young people who have an interest in art.

Ed White's career in football, as well as his second act, has been one long ride to greatness. But it hasn't all been greatness. Tragically, he lost his daughter in a car accident several years ago. "It has left a big hole in my heart," he says. "But I am looking forward to seeing her again and being with her someday."

Looking carefully at his athletic career and his commitment to his family and community, he has kept balance in his life. His daughter must be very proud of her father. Someday she will be able to tell him.

White and John Ward take a breather.

Sammy White beats the
Bears off the block.

Sammy WHITE

#85 | Wide Receiver, 1976–85

Fran Tarkenton likes to tell the story of how former Vikings head coach Jerry Burns gave Sammy White a bad time. A football player at Grambling, White also ran track and broke some of records set by the great Jesse Owens. "Burnsie used to tease Sammy all the time," remembers Tarkenton, "saying things like, 'Yeah, some record. Jesse Owens is 75 years old!'"

Kidding aside, Sammy White could run. Period.

White was born in Winnsboro, Louisiana, and grew up in Monroe. Growing up, he loved to play all sports. By the time he reached the seventh grade, he was an offensive guard and a defensive linebacker in football. In his sophomore year, he was a running back and then later wide receiver.

White had been an outstanding high school football player and pretty much could have picked where he wanted to go to college. He had earned high school All-American status for his accomplishments. "I had success in high school and was heavily recruited by many colleges, but I wanted to go to Grambling," says White.

"I saw a show on television about Grambling football and was really sold on the program," he remembers. "They had like eight guys from the program go on to play professional football. And then there was the fact that Eddie Robinson was at Grambling, and he was a tremendous coach and teacher. That was really important to me also. Once I got to know him, I found out what a great person he was both on and off the field. He didn't teach us just about football but about life.

"I loved playing at Grambling [but] never gave a thought early on to playing any pro football. I figured I got a football scholarship and that was enough for me. By the time I got to my senior year, I was doing well, and I started to give professional football some thought."

White was drafted by the Minnesota Vikings in the second round of the 1976 NFL Draft and was the 54th pick

> **"He was able to make cuts on the field like I had never seen before, and he had natural speed. He is…one of the best receivers I threw to in my career."**
>
> —FRAN TARKENTON

White keeps his eye on the ball.

overall. "I wasn't sure what was going to happen on draft day," White recalls. "Someone had to actually come and find me on campus. I just didn't want to stay by the phone and wait for it to ring."

As it turned out, White and Minnesota were a match made in heaven. He was off to the races in 1976, when he was named the NFL Offensive Rookie of the Year. During his career with the Vikings, he caught 393 passes for more than 6,400 total yards and 50 touchdowns. He was a two-time Pro Bowl selection and a three time All-Pro selection.

"I had some great years in Minnesota with the Vikings," recalls Sammy. "Early on, I recall spending too much time worrying about what the defensive backs were doing and not concentrating on catching the football, but I got it straightened out eventually. For me, it was lessons well learned.

"The Vikings....were a great organization, and there were not only great players but...wonderful teammates," he continues. "It was so exciting, and I enjoyed every minute of it...

"Fran Tarkenton was a tremendous help to me. He took me under his wing from day one and really worked to teach me the professional game. I recall him throwing ball after ball to me.... [He] was one of the smartest players, and what he did for me I greatly appreciated," says White.

Reflecting on those early days, White recalls the quarterback's perseverance. "I remember my very first touchdown in New Orleans. Fran ran back and forth across the field three times before he threw the ball to me."

Sammy White retired from football in 1985, after a long and successful NFL career. "It is a wonderful feeling to know that you are considered one of the best," says White. "It will be something my family will be able to look at forever.

"Now that football is over, my wife and I love to travel," says Sammy. "I like to garden and I also play a lot of racquetball and do a lot of walking. I follow all the sports on a regular basis—football, basketball, and baseball—but I am still in football as a coach at Grambling, one of my great passions."

White has now been the receivers coach at Grambling State University for 14 seasons. He worked with the team under head coach and former NFL quarterback Doug Williams, stayed on for a while when Williams left, and is now reunited with Williams again.

White was a legendary figure with the Tigers. As a collegiate player, he helped lead Grambling to three National Black College titles and three Southwestern Athletic Conference titles. As a senior he was named Co-Offensive Player of the Year in 1975. That pedigree, plus his experience as an NFL veteran, make him well suited as a role model for the young men who he coaches. "I truly love to give back to these players," he says. "It means a lot to me to assist them and to be at Grambling."

During White's coaching tenure, Grambling has won four more National Black College championships and four additional SWAC titles.

So, it has come full circle. Sammy White always wanted to play for Grambling, and he did in extraordinary fashion.

And with the Minnesota Vikings in the professional ranks, he was a standout receiver responsible for many big plays. He will always be remembered by the men who stood beside him, as well as in the hearts and minds of fans everywhere.

1976

In an incredible rookie season, White caught 51 passes for 906 yards and 10 touchdowns, third among receivers that year.

The Owners

Since the Wilf family took over ownership of the Minnesota Vikings in 2005, they have set a standard of high integrity. They have demonstrated a credibility and profound loyalty to both the community and former alumni players.

The Wilfs have vigorously worked to build a foundation of exceptional players and personalities for the future of the Minnesota Vikings. Through their strong leadership, they have designed a course with a long-reaching vision for the organization and Vikings fans. They also possess a deep, unwavering passion for the game and for the Minnesota Vikings legacy.

It was through this commitment that the 50 greatest Vikings team was conceived and created. It was a historic event in the history of the franchise and a fitting tribute to the team—past, present, and future.

Zygi and Mark Wilf at Arrowhead Stadium on October 2, 2011.

Mark Wilf (above) and Zygi Wilf (right) take in the pregame action at Mall of America Field.

Kevin WILLIAMS

#93 | Defensive Tackle, 2003–Present

Kevin Williams has been a dominant force on the defensive line for the Minnesota Vikings since his arrival in 2003. In each of his years with the organization, he has set a standard for excellence. Just don't expect him to tell you that. He is a lunch-bucket type of player who has little fanfare surrounding him; he simply goes about his business every day. Of course, his business happens to be causing pure mayhem on the football field.

"I grew up in Arkansas, a country boy," says Williams. "I was always involved in playing sports, and originally, I recall wanting to be a professional basketball player playing in the National Basketball Association. But realistically, I never gave a lot of thought to a specific career path."

In high school Williams played on the defensive line and also played tight end at Fordyce High School. He put up great numbers in several categories, which enabled him to get a scholarship and play at Oklahoma State.

Williams flourished at OSU, where he was a major force on the Cowboys defensive line and a starter in 42 games. During his collegiate career, he had 160 tackles, 38 of them tackles for losses. He played on the Oklahoma State team that made it to the Houston Bowl.

Kevin was drafted by the Minnesota Vikings in the first round of the 2003 NFL Draft, ninth overall. Since arriving in Minnesota, he has been selected to play in six Pro Bowls and has been named to the All-Pro Team on five occasions. He also made the 2000 All-Decade Team.

Williams was an impact player his very first year, leading the team in quarterback sacks with 10.5. He made the All-Rookie NFL Team and also received an award for

"Kevin is a pro's pro. He is an absolute joy to be with and to coach. He is tough, hard-nosed, a great teammate, super person, and players love to be around him. Kevin plays hard all the time and, although a quiet person, he is an exceptional leader. He sets a tremendous example, and when he speaks, you can literally hear a pin drop in the room."

—LESLIE FRAZIER

Kevin Williams stuffs Packers tight end Tom Crabtree.

All-NFL Rookie of the Month when he notched 18 tackles, five sacks of the quarterback, a forced fumble, and an interception in a four-game stretch. During the 2007 season, Williams had two interceptions, both of which he returned for touchdowns.

In addition to his football heroics, Williams has long been committed to giving back to the community: "I have been involved with the [Minnesota] Children's Hospital and really enjoy working with the kids there. It means a lot to me to be able to help in any way that I can.... We give out meals at Thanksgiving time, buy gifts.... During the off-season and in my spare time, I like to spend a lot of time... with my family in addition to my community work. It is all very important to me."

54.5

Williams has already notched 54.5 sacks in his career—and he's still going.

Kevin is also involved in a football-camp program. The camp's message for prospective campers reflects Williams' philosophy and how he has approached football and life:

"Players learn more than just football at camp. They are taught about teamwork, consideration of others, self-discipline, and how to attain their potential in sports and in life. Players also learn the importance of achieving good grades and selecting correct role models. We encourage them to go home a more positive, optimistic person."

Williams is a first-round draft pick who has lived up to his pre-draft hopes in so many more ways than one. He has been living proof on the field and off as well. He is a quiet, well-respected football player who has caused havoc among opposing team offenses for 10 seasons. Whether making a key tackle for a loss, sacking the quarterback, intercepting a pass, or just causing pure bedlam in jamming up the running game, he has been a performer week in and week out. He has also carried that commitment and tenacity with him into the community.

(Opposite) Williams breaks through the Detroit line. (Right) Getting some much-needed rest.

Winfield ends
the play with an
exclamation point.

Antoine WINFIELD

#26 | Cornerback, 2004–Present

Some say size matters, but Antoine Winfield is living proof that height, speed, and strength aren't the only measures of a football player's success. At just 5'9" and 190 pounds, Winfield looks a little out of place among his NFL counterparts. But make no mistake—he is a great football player and unassuming leader who achieved the highest successes in the professional game.

Talking about his childhood, growing up in Akron, Ohio, Winfield says, "I played a lot of football as a youngster. My hero was always Tony Dorsett of the Dallas Cowboys. He was such a great player. I played a lot of sandlot football at first, and then when I was about eight years old, we got into organized games.

"Even from a young age, I usually lined up at the safety position on defense, and I was a running back on the offensive side of the ball. I loved to play and loved the game."

Winfield was recruited by Ohio State after a standout high school career at Garfied High School in Akron. "John Cooper was the head coach at Ohio State at the time, and he recruited me heavily," recalls Winfield. "It was a good decision I made to go there. They had such a great football history with so many outstanding players who played their collegiate football there.

"I knew I wanted to excel in football and be able to play it for a long time. I have now played for 13 years in the National Football League and am still living the dream."

Winfield was a star player at Ohio State and won the Jim Thorpe Award and the Jack Tatum Trophy in 1998. In part because of the recognition he received for his outstanding college performance, he was selected in the first round of the 1999 NFL Draft by the Buffalo Bills, the 23rd pick overall.

Winfield remembers the electricity in the air on draft day: "We had a draft party. I thought I might be drafted high in the early rounds. And then I got the call from John Butler of the Bills in the first round. It was a real thrill for me."

Winfield played for the Bills from 1999 to 2003 before transitioning to the Minnesota Vikings as a free agent in 2004. With the Purple, he was named to the Pro Bowl in three consecutive years—2008–10—and was a First-Team All-Pro selection in 2008. Twice he was named National Football Conference Defensive Player of the Week.

"I have really enjoyed my time in Minnesota," Winfield says. "It is a great area to live in and has a tremendous school system. Mike Tice was the coach here when I arrived, and I have been very happy in all my years with the Vikings."

At this point in his NFL career, Winfield has developed into one of the very best defensive backs in the NFL. He is an outstanding position player and excellent tackler. Indeed, there is little question that he is one of the best and most aggressive tacklers in all of professional football. Despite his size, he has a reputation for being very physical.

As with many defensive backs, he is a big-play football player. While with the Vikings, he has been in the spotlight on numerous occasions. One of the biggest came on *Monday Night Football*, when he blocked a field goal and returned it 59 yards for a touchdown against the New Orleans Saints.

A college student, Winfield looks toward the future. *Photo courtesy of Antoine Winfield*

Winfield has three children and spends as much time as he can with his family during the season and especially in the off-season. "When I get some free time, I just like to relax and enjoy myself. We travel a lot. I have been to places such as Africa and China," he says.

"Overall, I am a real family person. I have a very strong value system that I have learned about life, and I want to instill it in my kids—things like be honest, never burn your bridges, don't talk badly about others, become a hard worker, and have a good time in life.... They are important messages to me, and I try to live by them every day."

Asked what the future may have in store for him once his playing days are through, Winfield says, "I'm not sure what I want to do when playing football is over, but I have thought about getting into coaching. I love the game and know I will miss it when I retire from playing."

Winfield seems to be living his life to the fullest, both professionally and personally. "I just enjoy life and have a good time at whatever I am doing. It's what is really important."

Talking about his selection to the Vikings 50, Winfield is grateful. He is one of only a handful of active players to have earned the distinction. "It is a very special honor for me," he says. "To be included along with all those great former Vikings means a great deal to me. To be recognized in that fashion for what I do for a living is incredible."

"Antoine has a great technique for making tackles, maybe the best in the history of the NFL. They should make a teaching film of his technique."

—JERRY BURNS

Cornerback is arguably one of the most difficult positions to play in the NFL. It is as grueling a position as there can be, and speed and size are crucial when the difference between good coverage is often measured in a single step. All of which makes Winfield's 13-year tenure all the more impressive. And in Winfield's case, he's only gotten better with age.

Most experts who follow football closely will say that Winfield is an underrated player. He is a good cover player and a great tackler. He simply can stop the run and the pass.

"He is a quiet leader and a real professional," says former teammate and All-Pro offensive guard Steve Hutchinson. Winfield's heart, determination, and remarkable play have won the respect of his teammates and fans alike.

24

You wouldn't expect it from a DB of his size, but Winfield has already wrestled away 24 interceptions in his NFL career.

Winfield readies for play in the September 25, 2011, game against the Detroit Lions.

Roy WINSTON

#60 | Linebacker, 1962–76

Roy Winston was seemingly there when it all began for the Minnesota Vikings some 50 years ago. He was also one of the original players who came on with the newly formed Minnesota Vikings in 1962, one year after the team's inaugural year in the National Football League.

He was a tough, hard-nosed linebacker who was known for his ferocious play, a Van Brocklin player from the old days who set the tone for what Vikings football was all about.

In his career, he wore only one jersey—the Vikings purple and gold—and he played in brilliant fashion for 15 straight years.

Winston was born and raised in Baton Rouge, Louisiana. "I went to Hollywood Elementary School as a kid," recalls Winston. "It was a Catholic school, and I remember way back then how much I enjoyed competing. We would have 'Sport Day' and have all kinds of competitive events in track and so forth. We had running events and the shot put among other things—and I wanted to win. I was pretty good at most things, and I remember getting a reward once: a candy bar."

But it wasn't just the promise of candy bars urging him on; Winston had an inborn competitive spirit. "Even at a very young age in elementary school, I was participating in football, basketball, and track," he says. "I carried those sports right into...Hollywood Junior High and to Istrouma High School. I recall making the varsity teams in the 10th grade and for a while was a halfback but then got switched into the line and played on both offense and defense as a defensive and offensive tackle.

"The great player Billy Cannon went to Istrouma High School and on to Louisiana State University, and I did the

"Roy was one of a great and formidable trio of linebackers for the Minnesota Vikings, along with Lonnie Warwick and Wally Hilgenberg. He was an outstanding player."

—FRAN TARKENTON

Winston was always in the middle of the action.

Winston wore the Purple with pride and honor.

"We call him 'Moonie'.... He was quick, very fast, and a real tough guy."

—MICK TINGELHOFF

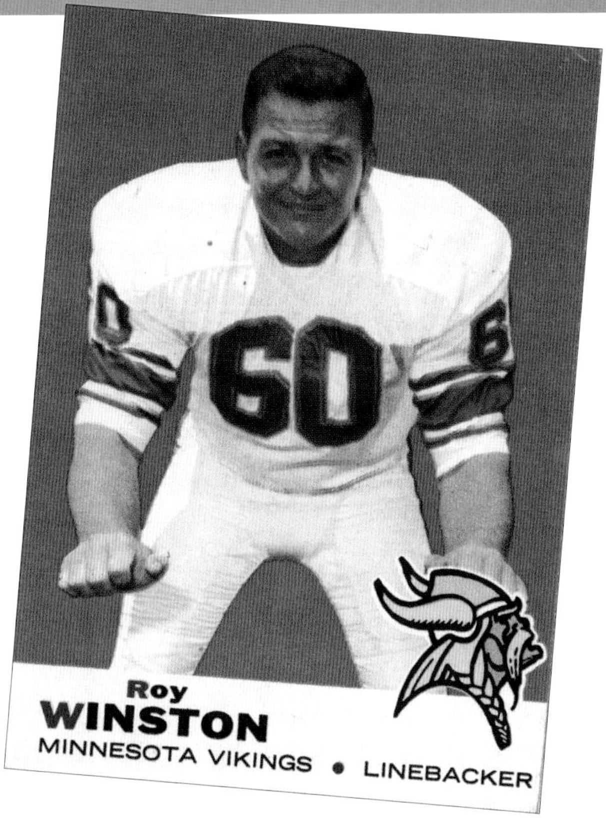

20

In his NFL career, Winston scored 20 points on three touchdowns and a safety. Not bad for a career defensive player.

same. Billy played for LSU from 1957 to 1959, and I got to LSU in 1958. I played offensive guard and defensive tackle in college." In 1976, Roy was inducted into the LSU Hall of Fame.

Winston earned All-American status at LSU. He was drafted by the Minnesota Vikings in the fourth round of the NFL Draft as the 45th overall pick.

Winston recalls those early days in Minnesota: "When I first came to the Vikings, head coach Norm Van Brocklin had me playing the linebacker position, and I was playing initially behind Rip Hawkins. By the next season, I was starting at outside linebacker—and that's where I stayed. It wasn't long before I was playing next to two of my greatest friends in Lonnie Warwick and Wally Hilgenberg. We played together as linebackers for many years.

"We used to all hunt and fish together. Many times we would go out in the woods or on the lakes before and after practice. And if we rode together, we always sat the same way we lined up on the field," recalls Roy.

Reflecting on the loss of his friend, Winston is sanguine. "When Wally died it was very difficult.... We played together for many years and did so many other things together, it's hard to think that he is gone," he says.

Winston returned to LSU in the off-season in order to get his degree. "I spent a lot of time in the real-estate business, worked in sporting goods, and worked for 25 years in sales for an oil service company. I was involved in quite a few things after I retired from football," says Winston.

For the most part, Roy is retired, spending plenty of his free time hunting and fishing. "It is something I really enjoy doing," Winston says.

Roy was humbled and pleased to be named one of the 50 greatest Vikings. "I was very honored and overwhelmed," says Roy. "It really means a lot to me to be among all of these great players."

He wore No. 60 and played the linebacker position for the Minnesota Vikings for 15 years. He was as tough as they come and was known for his bone-crushing hits and tackles. He was one of only 10 players who ended up playing in all four Super Bowls for the Vikings and was one of the men in Purple who set the table for what was to come in the future for the Vikings.

Roy Winston was a player's player, one who knew how to play the game with energy, spirit, and honor.

High school senior portrait.
Photo courtesy of Roy Winston

Yary lays a serious block against Saints pass rusher Derland Moore.

Ron YARY

#73 | Offensive Tackle, 1968–81

For 14 seasons, Ron Yary was an impenetrable force on the Vikings offensive line. When Minnesota went looking in 1968 for a big, aggressive offensive tackle, Yary fit the mold. One can almost imagine the talk in the back room of the Vikings offices after they drafted the great lineman. "Okay, we got Yary. Let's put him on the line, then we'll worry about the position in another 15 years or so."

Born in Chicago and raised in the Los Angeles area, Yary attended Bellflower High School. There he was an outstanding athlete, excelling in football, basketball, and baseball. And in case there's any doubt as to how good he was at the high school level, all one has to do is drive by the high school and see the football field at Ron Yary Stadium.

Reminiscing about his earliest sports memories, Yary says, "Baseball was one of my main interests growing up. I was too big to play at the organized football levels as a youngster. And I never considered playing professionally when I was younger. I just played sports because I loved the game. I never gave much thought at the time beyond what was happening on that particular day.

"As I got into college and really started to play well, my thoughts were to be patient and wait—even though I was really becoming a good player. I give a lot of credit to the school I went to in college, the University of Southern California. They did a good job of keeping the outside influences away from us. No one really talked much about a professional football career, whereas today, [most] kids go to college thinking about the professional football career."

While at USC, Yary was no less than a force for the Trojans. As a sophomore, he was voted the Pac-8 Defensive Lineman of the Year, as well as All–West Coast. In his junior year, coaches moved him from the defensive line to the offensive line. There, he was a consensus All-American, then a unanimous All-American in his senior year. He also won the Outland Trophy—as the nation's most outstanding lineman—and the Knute Rockne Award, another top lineman honor. In 1987, Ron Yary was inducted into the College Football Hall of Fame. He was also named to the ABC Sports, *Sports Illustrated,* and Walter Camp NCAA Football All-Century Teams.

But going to USC was about more than football for Yary. "Education was important to me," Yary insists, "and I got my business degree. After my eligibility was over, I never gave a thought to being picked high in the draft...until one of our coaches told me he thought that one of the teams was going to draft me as the first pick."

The coach was right, and Yary was the first player drafted in the 1968 NFL Draft. The Minnesota Vikings

Yary readies for the snap.

> **"Ron Yary is a Hall of Fame football player and the best blocker I have ever seen play the game of football."**
>
> —JERRY BURNS

had acquired the first pick from the New York Giants when they traded quarterback Fran Tarkenton to New York. Yary became the first offensive lineman to be selected as the No. 1 pick in the history of the draft. (To fully understand the magnitude of his abilities, consider that it was another 29 years before another offensive lineman was chosen at No. 1.) Luckily for Minnesota, he lived up to the billing.

During his years in Minnesota, Yary was a seven-time Pro Bowl selection and a six-time All-Pro. He was a two-time Second-Team All-Pro selection, an eight-time All-NFC choice, and a three-time National Football League Players Association NFC Offensive Lineman of the Year. He was selected for the NFL 1970s All-Decade Team.

7

Yary's seven Pro Bowl selections speak to his crucial contributions to the Vikings team.

In 2001, he was bestowed with the highest honor and recognition when he was inducted into the Pro Football Hall of Fame in Canton, Ohio.

"I had great years in Minnesota playing for the Vikings," recalls Yary. "I absolutely loved the Minneapolis–St. Paul area and really enjoyed the culture there. We had great teams in Minnesota [during] the years I played, and everyone got along well. It was fun to go to work. The coaches allowed us to play the game. When I played my last year with the Los Angeles Rams, things were very different. I realized how fortunate I was to have had the opportunity to play for the Minnesota Vikings for all of those years.

"The Vikings organization truly had respect for the players, from the coaches to management. It wasn't like that with many of the other teams. I had great respect for how the Vikings did their business. My offensive line coach, John Michels, and head coach Bud Grant were great to play for and be around. A perfect example of that was how we were treated when we traveled. The Rams would have the seats in the front of the plane sectioned off for the team management, while the Vikings had players sit near the front, depending on team seniority. We were simply respected as a part of the organization."

While wearing the Purple, Yary developed an interest that turned into a cottage industry for the player. "In the off-season, I got involved in photography work in 1974 with my brother, taking school photos and sports photography. We were working with 500 schools in California, taking their high school pictures."

These days, Ron keeps busy in semiretirement. He is involved with property-tax-based education, does charity work, and mentors high school football players. Being a husband and father and spending a lot of time with his family is also an important part of his world.

Ron Yary went from a first-round pick to one of the best linemen in the history of the game. He garnered practically every award that an offensive lineman could achieve. He played on 11 divisional title teams and played in four Super Bowls.

He was a very durable player and often played while injured. In fact, he only missed two games due to injury during his very long career. In 2000, the Vikings inducted him into the team's Ring of Honor. With a player like Yary, it's hard to choose which superlative is the greatest. All that is certain is that he is a part of the esteemed company that comprises the 50 greatest Vikings.

Yary, out of uniform but clad in Minnesota apparel, greets a young Vikings fan.

Vikings Unsung Heroes
Fred Zamberletti and Dennis Ryan

Together, they have served the Purple for a combined total of 89 seasons. The words *trust*, *honesty*, *integrity*, *credibility*, and *loyalty* are their trademarks. They are special people with hearts of gold traced in purple. Fred Zamberletti and Dennis Ryan are two of the most beloved people in the history of the Vikings. Just ask anyone in the organization. These two men's commitments to the game and the franchise have been unparalleled.

Fred Zamberletti was the athletic trainer for the Minnesota Vikings from 1961 to 2003. He continues with the team as a consultant and team historian. Fred attended 1,047 consecutive games from the inception of the franchise to 2011, before missing his first contest. In 43 seasons with the organization as the athletic trainer, he never missed a single day of work. He was inducted into the Ring of Honor on December 20, 1998, and has been a franchise cornerstone for half a century.

The team equipment manager, **Dennis Ryan**, just completed his 36th season with the Minnesota Vikings. He was promoted to the position in 1981, when he was just 21 years old. He is only the second person in Vikings history to hold claim to the position. Ryan is the original inventor of the helmet visor that has now become a common piece of equipment in the National Football League. He remains one of the veteran equipment managers in the NFL, and his devotion and commitment to perform at the highest level is second to none.

Fred Zamberletti

Dennis Ryan

Gary ZIMMERMAN

#65 | Offensive Tackle, 1986–92

Gary Zimmerman received the ultimate football honor when he was inducted into the Pro Football Hall of Fame in Canton, Ohio, with fellow members from the Class of 2008. But the road to Canton was paved with plenty of blood, sweat, and tears along the way.

Raised in Fullerton, California, Zimmerman played sports at Walnut High School. "I had it in my mind from a very young age that I wanted to play professional football," he says. "And as I got older, I never wavered from it. It is what I wanted to do."

Those around him were, perhaps, less enthusiastic. "I didn't have a lot of encouragement from a lot of people as far as what I was going to accomplish," he continues. "I can recall being told things like, I would never be good enough to play a down in college, let alone in the professional ranks. But I worked at it. I spent a lot of time in the weight room and I studied the game.

"I probably had above-average talent for the game, however my time lifting weights really helped me. In many ways, I think back then I was probably ahead of my time by some of the things I did to prepare for the game. I had smarts for the game because I really worked at it. I watched a lot of film and didn't just focus my study on the opposing players, but all the aspects of the game…. Not many [high school] players were doing that kind of thing, so I was very well prepared."

After a stellar high school career, Zimmerman attended the University of Oregon, where his play earned him admission into the Oregon Sports Hall of Fame in 2002. Gary was a three-year letterman at Oregon and is ranked as one of the best offensive linemen to ever play there. He was named the Pac-10 Offensive Lineman of the Year in his senior year and was awarded the prestigious Morris Trophy.

"Gary Zimmerman is the best technician of the game of football that I have ever been around. He was an even-keeled player who had great skills and was one of the best offensive tackles to play the game."

—SCOTT STUDWELL

Zimmerman keeps QB Wade Wilson safe.

"Zimmerman is a Hall of Famer. He was a tremendous offensive tackle in the National Football League and played the game with great technique."

—JERRY BURNS

Hall of Famer Gary Zimmerman: the man, the myth, the mustache.

184

Zimmerman started in 184 games in his outstanding NFL career, playing in postseason contests with both the Vikings and the Broncos.

After being drafted in the first round of the supplemental draft in 1984 by the New York Giants, Zimmerman elected instead to play his first two years in professional football with the Los Angeles Express of the United States Football League, where he was a two-time All-USFL player. Following his USFL stint, he was traded to the Minnesota Vikings in 1986, where he remained until 1992. (He went on to finish his career with the Denver Broncos.)

During Zimmerman's time in the professional ranks, he was selected for the Pro Bowl seven times and was a five-time All-Pro selection and a three-time Second-Team All-Pro selection. He was also named to NFL's 1980s All-Decade Team and the 1990s All-Decade Team, a rare double feat.

While with the Vikings, Zimmerman started 169 consecutive games. He was an outstanding run blocker and pass blocker on the offensive line and had a great understanding of the game.

Reflecting on a big change in his career momentum, Zimmerman says, "One of the real blessings in my career was when I was switched from the offensive center/guard positions to the offensive tackle spot. I was suited well for the position, and it was great for my career."

Today, he speaks of his time in Minnesota with fondness. "I lived in the Eden Prairie area when I played for the Vikings. It was like a second family for me, and I had a great relationship with my teammates. I played with some really outstanding football players, like Randall McDaniel, Terry Tauch, Tim Irwin, and so many others.... And coach John Michels was very special to me also."

Like many of his fellow Vikings, Zimmerman is a natural outdoorsman. "Minnesota was also a great area for two of my other passions: fishing and hunting. There are so many wonderful areas with all the lakes," recalls Gary.

Today, he lives the country life, settled in his home deep in the woods. He devotes some of his time to football camp for high schoolers. He uses his own life experiences to teach and inspire the youngsters. "When you know what you want to do in life, you have to go for it," says Zimmerman. "And in the process, you must do things the right way on and off the field."

He was a solid outstanding football player, one who achieved great honors and awards for his contributions on the football field but never forgot those who helped him along the way. "John Randle and Chris Doleman put me in the Hall of Fame," he says, "because I had to line up and play against them every day in practice. I had no choice. All I could do was get better."

Acknowledgments

I want to express my deepest gratitude and sincere appreciation to Bob Hagan, director of public relations for the Minnesota Vikings. Without the help of Bob and his commitment to assist me from the very beginning of this process, this book on the 50 greatest Vikings would never have become a reality. I also want to thank Brad Madson, Tom West, Eric Haigh, and Jon Ekstrom of the Vikings for their dedicated commitment in providing photos of the team and its greatest players.

To the members of the Vikings 50 who agreed to be interviewed, thank you for your generosity in sharing your memories as well as your personal photos for this book.

My special appreciation also goes to my wonderful friend, Hall of Fame quarterback Fran Tarkenton, for his willingness to spend the time and energy to write the exceptional foreword to this book. Thank you, Fran!

I want to say thank you to my publisher, Triumph Books in Chicago, and all of their superior staff who have assisted me in my third book with the organization. A special thanks to Mitch Rogatz, Tom Bast, Don Gulbrandsen, Adam Motin, Noah Amstader, and Katy Sprinkel, my editor.

A special thanks goes to the Wilf Family and to the entire Vikings organization, for putting together and supporting the concept of the 50 greatest Vikings team. They have banked an incredible memory for all of us who have fallen in love with the team over the past five decades.

Finally, a special thank you to my beloved family, who have always provided me with their magnificent love and support.